GW01018522

99 Park Street

Ian Anthonisz

Clink
Street

London | New York

Published by Clink Street Publishing 2018

Copyright © 2018

First edition.

The author asserts the moral right under the Copyright, Designs and Patents Act 1988 to be identified as the author of this work.

All rights reserved. No part of this publication may be reproduced, stored in a retrieval system or transmitted, in any form or by any means without the prior consent of the author, nor be otherwise circulated in any form of binding or cover other than that with which it is published and without a similar condition being imposed on the subsequent purchaser.

ISBN: 978-1-912562-63-3 paperback
978-1-912562-64-0 ebook

Acknowledgements

My thanks goes to all the following people who played a big part in getting me to this stage of the game and who had an influence in shaping my life.

My mother who made the decision to emigrate to the UK.

My paternal uncle Edward Anthonisz, who I would say gave me the greatest insight into common sense thinking.

The institution of St Thomas' College and the excellent teaching staff there at the time.

The special members of staff of Woodberry Down, Mrs Chetwynd, Major John Biginell and Ken Dyos for their faith in my ability

Mr Reginald Murley the consultant surgeon who was brought in on the weekend to save my life after the car crash I was involved in.

Mr Ivor Smith, the surgeon who helped stitch me up and assisted Mr Murley, during the operation to save my life.

Janice who worked so hard to assist me establish my business and particularly at the beginning to ensure we would succeed and for her constant support over the years.

All my immediate family for the support and encouragement they game to complete this book

My sincere thanks to both my good friends Peter Nicol and Bob Dobbs who gave me the pictures and illustrations in this book and helps the reader to visualise some parts of this story

Dedication

I dedicate this book to the memory of the late Kenneth Hume who was the single person whom through nothing but his kindness started me on the road to fulfilling my business and personal ambitions and the ultimate success that I think I achieved.

I also undertake to donate 10% of the sales proceeds of this book to our charity "Once in a lifetime" (www.oialcharity. org.uk)

Contents

1.

Introduction and Background

This book sets out the personal story of the author, Ian Anthonisz, a first generation immigrant to the United Kingdom from Ceylon, now Sri Lanka, who was a 'Burgher boy' – these were people of Dutch decent, and the word 'Burgher' comes from the Dutch word for 'citizen'. Ian and his parents left their home country, Ceylon, now called Sri Lanka, in search of a new life in England because they feared for the future prospects of their children in their own homeland.

Ceylon was going through some fundamental political changes, which to the Burgher community signified future turmoil, after the then Prime Minister S W R D Bandaranaike decided to change the official and first language in Ceylon from English to Sinhala, thereby creating the well-known Sinhala-only policy of Ceylon, at that time.

The Burghers were a minority community in Ceylon and originated from Dutch and Portuguese settlers. The dutch arrived in Galle, which is at the south-western tip of the island in 1670 and established the Galle Fort, which still stands there today. Galle has now become one of the most fashionable places to live in Sri Lanka having an expanding ex-pat community, with property prices there being on par with those of central London.

Once the language change took place in Ceylon, the Burgher community at large felt that their lack of being able to communicate in Sinhala would put them at a distinct disadvantage and therefore as a whole they decided to seek a future abroad.

After the Dutch period, Ceylon had been a colony of the British for around 150 years until independence in 1948, and therefore the obvious first choice was England simply because it was the capital of the Commonwealth and was the place most associated with English, their language, as well as the educational background and, of course, the all-important link to the mother country.

Having said that, the climate of Europe was not the most inviting to people who were born and lived in Ceylon, which is an island close to the equator and has a wonderful climate all year round, drenched in sunshine and with beautiful beaches together with an even temperature of 28C to 31C most of the time – therefore many Burghers who managed to fulfil the criteria of the Australian all-white immigration policy which existed in the 1950s, opted for the warmer shores of Australia. Under the all-white policy any Burgher applicants had to prove their European origin (Australia immigration act 1901).

The other factors which favoured England as a destination was the worldwide recognition of an English education and qualifications, which appealed to many of the Burghers who had already been educated in the private schools of Ceylon. These were modelled on the public school system of

Britain and were still much sought after. Strangely enough, Prime Minister Bandaranaike, the author of the Burgher outflow from Ceylon, was educated at St Thomas' College one of the leading private schools in Ceylon, modelled on Winchester public school in England. He then graduated at Oxford University and was himself the President of the Oxford Union.

Aside from England and Australia fewer number of Burghers sought a future in Canada and the United States as well, probably dictated by either family connections or job offers which came to the persons concerned. In any case it was to a far smaller extent than England or Australia. However, when in the mid-sixties the Australian immigration policy was relaxed, many of the Burghers seized the opportunity and went there, mostly settling in all the big cities such as Melbourne, Sydney, Brisbane, Adelaide and Perth, where a previously settled relative was able to sponsor them. There were also some in places as far north as Darwin, which were attractive to some of the professionals such as teachers and doctors because of tempting job offers.

In the case of Ian Anthonisz, the decision was made easier because his aunt (his mother's sister) had already migrated to Britain and had lived there for approximately two years, and the temptation of joining this connection was a major factor. In addition, his stepfather was of Tamil origin, another minority community in Ceylon, and he also felt the same impending turmoil in the motherland.

After the pros and cons were analysed by his parents the decision to move to England was taken. The family including Ian, his brother David and half-brother Darrell moved to London to begin their new life adventure.

Ian's story, tells how as a young immigrant boy he started a new life with little or no financial backing and managed to get accepted into British society at the highest level, and also worked his way into one of the treasured and closed professions of the day, that of chartered accountancy, and through hard work and dedication – together with more than a few twists of fate or destiny coupled with good fortune – he managed to found his own accountancy practice in the West End of London to compete with the best. His nucleus of clients included a cross-section of business entrepreneurs, owner-operated companies, professionals and of course some high net-worth individuals from all sections of British society. He says that he was lucky enough to meet these clients, some of whom were well known celebrities in England and this contributed to his being able to build a niche practice and mix socially with some sections of elite British society

In addition, as a side-line, he built up a successful property business and although he may not have been another Richard Branson, his story serves as an example to any ambitious young entrepreneurs that it is possible to achieve success from where ever you start and to be able to compete with the best.

He also ventured into the world of IT software when he originated a bookkeeping and accounting program, using the practical experience he had gained over the years in his accountancy practice. Ian always says that one must look at any service from an 'end users' point of view, something he has tried to achieve in all his business enterprises.

2.

Beginnings of Life in the Business World

The prestigious offices of chartered accountants Stoy Hayward were at 99 Park Street, Mayfair London. I knew that inside the large wide polished wooden door were the lush offices of one of the leading firms of West End accountants in England and here I was, a first generation young immigrant from Ceylon who was going to begin my career in accountancy

Before I walked in through the door I pondered a while, thinking about how I got here in the first place and was now on the brink of starting a career in a profession that I knew little or nothing about. My thoughts went back to how I met my benefactor Kenneth Hume who played a major player in my early life in England and to how we decided that I was going to become a chartered accountant. It took me all the way back to the sequence of events and the all-important first meeting with Kenneth Hume that eventually led to this scenario in the first instance.

I have always been someone whose life path has been changed by what I can only describe as the toss of a coin syndrome, not that this does not apply to others but in my case there has been no long preplanning for the sudden changes that have happened, partly due to my own personality and character. This phenomenon can be seen throughout this story and the sequence of events that follow at almost every juncture and change of direction, both for good or bad throughout my account of events.

Starting with how I met Kenneth Hume and the influence he had on my early life in England is truly fascinating and uncanny and needs to be recorded both for future reference, as the phenomenon I mentioned earlier and what I refer to as the luck of life, fate, destiny or whatever one calls it and can work either way. Some refer to it as being in the right or wrong place at the right time. This has been repeated in my case throughout most of my life, and while I am sure must be the case with most of us – it seems that some of us grab at it as an opportunity and others chose to ignore it, which in turn changes our whole life story – it seems to have had an overriding bearing on life for me. Perhaps it is only because I wish to think of it that way.

I need to start by going back to the day I arrived in England to begin this part of the story. Having arrived in Tilbury on a cloudy damp August day after a twenty-one day voyage from Colombo in sunny Ceylon on board the SS *Orsova*, the flagship of the P&O line passenger fleet at the time, with my mother and two brothers David and Darrell. We were here to seek a new life in England.

Having disembarked from the ocean liner, we travelled from the port of Tilbury in Essex to Stamford Hill in North London where we were went to live on a temporary basis with my mother's sister auntie Dorothy and my cousin Wendy. They had arrived here almost two years or so earlier from Ceylon and were the mentors of our own family, moving at that time to England.

Once we got there, we were welcomed with the usual family greetings and advice of how to start our new life and to make the best of this new start we began settle in as best as possible. Later on that first afternoon, I telephoned an ex- school friend of mine, Maurice Rode. He had been in school with me but had left Colombo some eighteen months earlier to live in London. The purpose of my call was to surprise him with an announcement that I was in London and I wanted to check out if we could meet up on the next day, my second day in England. Maurice greeted me with total surprise and said, "Of course, I would love to see you, but I am going for an audition for some kind of a film part in the morning. I can meet you afterwards." My answer was that it would be easier if I met him at the place of the audition and we could go out together from there, after his appointment… he agreed.

The audition was in Wardour Street in the centre of Soho, where it all happened in the film world in those days and when I arrived at the offices of Kenneth Hume productions there was a queue of several hundred people waiting to go in. Not being one of the interviewees I walked straight up the stairs and asked at reception if my friend Maurice Rode was already there. I was told that he had arrived and was being auditioned by Mr Kenneth Hume and that I would have to take a seat and wait for him. I sat quietly in the seat I was given and after about fifteen minutes Maurice came out accompanied by a person, to whom I was introduced to as being the film producer Kenneth Hume. Maurice's introduction of me while pointing me out was, "This is my friend Ian from Ceylon; he has come here to meet me." At this point Kenneth Hume asked me if I also was a Burgher to which I replied "Yes." As explained earlier a Burgher is a Ceylonese term for a person of Dutch or Portuguese origin and the burghers had a particular accent which Kenneth Hume wanted.

He immediately said, "In that case you had better have an audition as well." Needless to say, I immediately agreed and all three of us went back into the auditorium. I took the test that Maurice had already taken and most surprisingly Kenneth Hume turned to both of us and said, "I want both of you to be at Merton Park studios at nine o'clock on Monday morning, please see this lady who will give you your contracts."

To say that I was excited at this totally unexpected and unsolicited success on my second day in the country is the biggest understatement to say the least, but little did I know at this moment how this chance meeting with Kenneth Hume would have such a permanent and long-lasting bearing on my entire life, and all the things that it would eventually lead to. The voiceover contract was a big break enough for anyone, let alone two seventeen-year-old boys from Ceylon. The contract provided that both Maurice and I would get five pounds a day for every day we worked, that at a time when the average weekly wage for an ordinary working man was around six to eight pounds. We were both very lucky, I would say, very lucky indeed.

During the filming and voiceover process, both Maurice and I became extremely good friends with the film crew and the rest of the cast and of course with Kenneth Hume himself. He was an extremely kind and generous man and we soon discovered that he not only loved Ceylon but had adopted a blind boy there when he was making the original film about a year or so earlier, and always referred to him as his son. He was also a person who took an interest in the people around him. It was in one of the breaks in work he asked about how we managed as new immigrants to a country after having a comparatively easy and comfortable life in Ceylon. I replied that it was hard for us as a family as my mother had not worked at home and had to take whatever work was available in a clothing factory in order to establish ourselves here.

Kenneth Hume offered me a Saturday job to wash his car, a sporty Volkswagen Karmann Ghia, an offer that I jumped at, bearing in mind that I wanted to make a contribution to the family budget. This little part-time job carried on for a very long time afterwards throughout which Kenneth Hume was extremely generous financially.

It was on one of these Saturdays after I had washed his car and was having a cup of coffee with him that he asked me if I had any idea of what job I was going to do after leaving school, to which I replied that I was trying to get an engineering apprenticeship with a big company. He asked if I had any luck so far, to which I replied that I had done over forty-three applications and had no offers of an interview at all. He said "Do you think that this is due to any racial or colour prejudice of any kind?" Racial or colour prejudice was a subject that was quite talked about at that time. I replied that I did not know and he said, "That must have been very depressing either way."

The next Saturday when I met Kenneth Hume he said, "Ian you need you to make a formal application to Rolls Royce for an apprenticeship as I have spoken to someone I know there and he gave me the name of Major General G A Bond as the person I had to contact. Guess what? I was given an interview with them and had to visit the company to meet the Major General himself at the factory of the truck division of Thorneycroft's in Hants. Once again I could not believe my ears at the change of fate that had taken place – from zero responses to all my applications to an interview at the truck division of Rolls Royce

The train journey to the factory was most thought-provoking in as much that the chance meeting with Kenneth Hume on day two in England had set me on my way to my desired career in mechanical engineering, a twist of fortune totally out of my control.

The meeting with Maj. Gen. Bond went off very well and so did my tour of the factory with him. I duly had a letter of confirmation of the offer of a place with them, conditional of my getting two GCE A-level passes. Here I was about to begin a career in engineering with the Rolls Royce Group… Was I dreaming?

Normally engineering apprentices with Rolls Royce would need to have a degree in one of the engineering faculties at a good university and, as Maj. Gen. Bond; explained to me GCE A-levels were a modest qualification. Having just arrived here from Ceylon I was not aware of the subtlety of the English idiom despite my very good basic education at St Thomas' College in Mount Lavinia, Colombo, Ceylon.

We as 'Thomians' – students of St Thomas' – came from what was considered to be the finest boy's school there. To be a Thomian was not just an education, but a fellowship like no other, and my education at St Thomas' was to be one of the greatest assets that I brought with me to England. More about that later on.

I carried on with the A-level course for almost two years, but realised that maths at that level was not my greatest subject and one afternoon on the way home from school, almost as an impulse, decided that perhaps a career in business rather than engineering may be the better option for me. The one thing I knew all along was that I always wanted to be a 'Boss' rather than an underdog. This meant that I never wanted to end up on an engineering work bench, so a career in business is what was right for me and that is what I decided to go for… A total change of course and direction!

What about Rolls Royce, Maj. Gen. Bond and Kenneth Hume? All of whom had taken time and effort to get me to where I already was. Well, in short, I had a problem and it needed to be sorted out. I have never been scared or slow in making a decision, even to this day people around me accuse me of making decisions too quickly; the truth is that I prefer to make a decision and change it if I have to, rather than think about it so long that the opportunity passes.

There was only one thing to do, I walked into the nearest phone box and dialled Kenneth Hume. When he answered, somewhat in trepidation I said, "Mr Hume do you remember me? Ian Anthonisz – you got me fixed up as an apprentice at Rolls Royce; well I am not sure I want to do engineering any longer." His response was abrupt and somewhat unexpected. "I seem to spend all my time finding other people jobs these days without making any money for myself." All I could muster was "Err… sorry Mr Hume, I did not mean to trouble you, it does not really matter." There was a short silence and then he said, "Sorry Ian, I did not mean to dismiss you so abruptly, come and see me at my new home in Westbourne Terrace and you can explain the problem to me." That was a relief indeed and almost immediately, I returned to my normal optimistic self.

When I arrived at Westbourne Terrace a few days later as arranged, I walked up the short pathway to the front door and, hesitating a little, pushed the buzzer and waited for a moment or so. A shadow appeared against the semi-frosted glassed door and it was opened by an impeccably groomed butler. Kenneth Hume must have become more successful and wealthy since I last met him, I thought. Can I help you he asked? I replied that I was Ian Anthonisz and had an appointment with Mr Hume. The butler said Mr Hume is on his way back from his office but is expecting you, do come in and wait for him. I walked in as invited and was led into the lounge, a large room furnished mostly in white with big chairs and curious artefacts.

I looked around curiously for the mounted leopard skin that I had sold him soon after I had met him, during the voiceover production; in fact it was my first business deal in England. Auntie Dorothy had a leopard skin which was beautifully mounted after her husband had shot a leopard in Ceylon on a game shoot, which of course was the fashion before animal rights were even born, and she had brought this to England. I remembered that she was interested in selling it. I knew that Kenneth Hume was keen on collecting such things and as it had come up in conversation, so I asked my aunt how much she wanted for it? She said, "Ian if you can get me eight pounds for it, I will be over the moon."

I said I would try to get that for her and duly asked Kenneth Hume how much he would pay for a mounted leopard's head. He said that he would be happy to get one for ten pounds, a clear profit of 25% for my trouble and interest, all parties to the deal were ecstatic at the outcome.

Kenneth Hume duly arrived home and after pouring some drinks and some polite exchanges, we got talking.

"Well," he said, "what is this all about? You don't want to be an engineer after all, so what do you want to do?" I explained the problem with advanced maths and my fear of ending up on the work bench. "What do you want to be?" I explained that I wanted to have a career in business, something like be a business manager, which could lead eventually to a directorship or other senior position. He immediately retorted, "How about banking? I know the president of the bank of America, I am sure I could get you in there." I had to hold myself in the chair, this was far too easy and beyond any of my expectations. I replied, "Sure that sounds amazing to me." He immediately picked up the phone and dialled a number, the phone rang for a few minutes and he said, "Looks like he is out for the evening." A few sips of scotch later he said, "What about a chartered accountant?" To be totally honest I didn't know what exactly that was, but I knew it was an important career because my father always walked around the accountant's room in his office with some awe and trepidation whenever my brother and I visited his office in the Ceylon Civil Service.

I said, fine I will give it a go… Kenneth Hume immediately dialled another number, explaining to me that David Gubbay was a very respected show business accountant and he was sure he could get me into his practice as a trainee. Once again, the phone rang for a few minutes. "Looks like he is out as well." Had fate dealt me a negative blow? I pondered that, nobody of any influence was in that evening, how was it all going to end for me in the career stakes? I wondered nervously about the final outcome. After a few minutes of further thought Kenneth Hume assured me that all was not lost and it was merely a temporary setback that nobody was in that evening

He told me that he would be in touch with me as soon as he could; I was to go home and not worry about it because he knew many people in business and he would surely get back to me with some news in no more than a few days. Feeling quite reassured I set off on my journey home pondering all the possible opportunities. I had to admit that I felt a tinge of anticipation and excitement all the way home.

It was a few days before I heard and I was getting somewhat anxious at the lack of news, but then an official letter arrived addressed to me, marked for my personal attention; I opened it with a mixture on anxious excitement and trepidation as I did not know what it would contain. It read "Dear Ian, I have spoken to Edward Langton, the senior partner of Stoy Hayward etc. etc. who will give you an interview with the intention of taking you on as an articled clerk, I want you to phone his secretary and make an appointment to see Mr Langton etc. etc. There was a typed PS: "Please don't forget to look very smart and smile when you go to the interview and meet Mr Langton and good luck". The letter ended with a handwritten note: "Dictated by and sent in the absence of Kenneth Hume"

I was overjoyed with the news the letter contained and could barely contain myself until it was possible to phone Mr Langton's secretary, Marion Robb She knew all about the arrangements and the entire process from there on it was a mere formality. We live in a very strange world

I thought, I had made over forty applications without so much as an acknowledgement and yet one word from one friend to another and I had an interview arranged in a matter of minutes with the senior partner of a leading West End firm of chartered accountants.

The interview was even more of a revelation as to how the system can work for you if you happen to be on the right side of the game. I arrived for my interview, walked into the plush offices of Stoy Hayward, and presented myself to a very glamourous looking receptionist who looked more as if she was out of the cast of a James Bond film than an accountant's office. I was asked to take a seat until Miss Robb arrived; I did so and waited. It wasn't long until a tall extremely well dressed Scottish lady, Marion Robb, arrived in the lift. She greeted me as though I was somebody important and she took me upstairs to meet Mr Langton.

The interview lasted just a few minutes, beginning with "Anthonisz, How did you get to know Kenneth Hume?" I told him the short version of the story and a few questions later Edward Langton offered me the position of being one of his articled clerks, a distinct privilege, I thought. He said "Starting 4th August." I replied that I could start earlier as I was finishing school in the June. He said, "Take the opportunity of a long holiday because you won't get another long one for five years." The interview was over in a relatively short time and I was officially on the way to becoming a chartered accountant.

This was certainly my introduction of how the old boys' network worked in England. I was quite used to this in Ceylon where people knew other well-connected people in a much smaller country and community. Apart from that everyone who went to St Thomas' college, where I was educated, was connected by the fellowship and all 'Thomians' – as we were called past and present – had this old boys' network. I was an old Thomian, as was my father and my grandfather before him, and so were the first four prime ministers of post-independence Ceylon. Also as I was growing up my father seemed to know everyone of any importance as they were in school with him. You can therefore get the measure of how things worked in that country, but in somewhere as big as England, well it was another lesson that I learned very fast and never forgot both in my personal and business – life is all about who you know rather than what.

The time after my successful interview and the start date of my articleship at Stoy Hayward was to be filled with my A-level exams and the end of my school career, which started at St Thomas' College, Mount Lavinia in Ceylon and was to end at Woodberry Down School in North London. Both institutions did play a great part in the formation of my sense of values and my approach to life in general, because of the particular situations of my childhood and the move to another country in the middle of school life.

St Thomas' was an institution of over a hundred years old with many traditions and a history covering the colonial period of English Ceylon and of course the early years of independence. Like many English public schools, the head teacher was the ultimate power and as boys we walked in trepidation of his presence.

All the head teachers – save the head of my day, Canon Reginald de Saram – were of English origin and had belonged to the priesthood. The school had a strong tradition of fellowship and discipline second to none. The schools motto was 'Esto Perpetua' (Be Thou Forever) so one can imagine the type of value it instilled in any boy who was a pupil.

In Ceylon to have been educated there was in itself a life-long qualification and at that time was considered to be a passport for life, added to which if you had been in the first team for cricket or rugby, then you simply were the 'bees knees' of your time.

Woodberry Down School on the other hand although it was a normal secondary school in North London, was the first Mixed Comprehensive School brought in by the Labour Party and was quite by accident the flagship of the education policy at that time. The head teacher was a woman named Mrs Chetwynd, the wife of a senior Labour MP and all the heads of department and the assistant teachers were handpicked to ensure that the comprehensive system would succeed.

My brother David and I benefitted by this simply because we happened to be in the right place at the right time.

Both David and I fitted in very easily, simply because of our background at St Thomas' and in what was a few weeks were able to get places in the cricket and rugby teams without too much of a struggle, something which we would not have been able to achieve so easily at St Thomas', as the competition and the standard would have been infinitely greater.

David and I were the new boys there and because of our transfer to the UK as teenagers went straight into the fifth and sixth forms respectively and of course got known to the teachers and pupils on somewhat of a fast-track method. In addition the competitive spirit instilled in us at St Thomas' made us go for everything that was available and for the taking, resulting in David becoming a prefect and me a senior prefect in our very first year there. David later went on to become the head boy of the school, a great privilege as he had to make the head boy speech to the guest of honour on prize-day, someone no less than Mary Rand MBE, the Olympic gold medallist

Our spell at Woodberry Down, two years in my case and three years for David, marked a turning point in our lives in our new country of residency because when we decided to leave Ceylon I had got to a point in my school life where I had suffered a loss of and interest in study and had very little desire to achieve academic success. I was at the point of cashing in on the school's reputation and going into one of those professions which needed some technical skills, but relied more on personality and PR skills rather than academic success. These were jobs such as tea tasting, tea planting, etc. It was basically a job that required few qualifications and more of school and family connections, and I could hardly wait to leave college and get on with it. In fact, our emigration to the UK gave both David and me a shot in the arm as far as new interests and academic ambitions went.

My uncle, who was my father's elder brother and a head teacher himself, advised that we seek to get into Woodberry Down School in North London because it was a new school and was a showcase comprehensive, and the calibre of the teaching staff were all exceptional because they were hand-picked for their quality by the Mrs Chetwynd, the head teacher. We first met with this lady in her office and after an initial conversation she invited the senior housemaster, Major John Biginell to meet with us there. At that stage neither of us realised what a huge part he would play in the rest of our school lives and in the case of my brother David, long after he left school and for many years into his later career.

The fact that we were at fifth-year stage and new arrivals from abroad gave us this very personal introduction, which all the normal pupils would not have had. Major Biginell had a reputation for being a strict disciplinarian and was in charge of the strict running of the school, he also ran the schools Duke of Edinburgh's Award Scheme, which had of course only started a few years earlier in any part of the world; again this would provide some very important kudos for both of us in the next year or so.

John Biginell seemed to take a liking to both of us and gave us our respective initiations of the school and looked at us over the top rim of his glasses as he spoke to us very sternly and deliberately, as he always did in his official capacity. He then gave us the School House to which we both were to belong to. This as a matter of interest this was Scott House' named after the famed explored Robert Falcon Scott of Antarctic fame.

Since that meeting in the senior housemaster's room, John Biginell started what we always considered to be a special relationship with us. I say this because whenever he wanted to pick volunteers for a specific task in the school he always included David and me. This culminated about two months later by making both David and me into school prefects.

As prefects he charged all of us with helping him to maintain order in all school matters, such as entry and exit into the school building at all points, morning assembly and such matters. I think that this process may have been a major contributory factor in how I approached my early business tasks and eventually how I ran my own company. The influence of John Biginell was a long lasting and great one.

A few days after we started in Woodberry Down, we taken by John Biginell and introduced to Mr Ken Dyos, the head of the maths department and the form teacher of the sixth form – he was to be our personal tutor in our school life thereafter. Once again this introduction seemed to be a twist of fate that would have far-reaching consequences to our lives in England.

Ken Dyos was a man of great academic stature. He was a Master of Science and a fellow of the Royal Society of Science; he too was hand-picked to head the maths department at Woodberry Down. He was one of the most valued members of Mrs Chetwynd's senior staff and, like John Biginell, seemed to like both David and me, for whatever reason, we shall never know.

I need to mention that at this stage of my educational life I was totally uninterested in maths and in fact before I left St Thomas' in Ceylon had taken a mock exam in maths for which I only achieved 2½% in total. I thought about this failure many times and felt that I must have been given those marks for neat handwriting only. This aside, Ken Dyos sparked a new interest in the subject for me, and only four months later I passed my GCE O-level in ten subjects including both Pure Maths and Additional Pure Maths, something which six months earlier would have been an impossible, even unthinkable feat. This was a measure of the man and his dedication to teaching. It also taught me something even more important, which was that if one was interested enough in anything, then achieving any goal was completely possible, I have never forgotten this and have used it in many aspects of my life and in inspiring both clients staff and others alike.

Life at Woodberry Down was truly amazing for both of us both academically and in all other areas of our lives. In sport we were in the cricket and rugby teams and were making great strides in the Duke of Edinburgh's Award Scheme and getting recognition from both staff and fellow students alike. At the end of this academic year both of us achieved at least ten O-levels each.

I would like to recall an incident that finally cemented the relationship between John Biginell and me. I was on pre-fect duty in one of the school corridors at the end of one lunch-time and the third year pupils were walking through to their classrooms. Our task was to keep them silent and in line as they went to their respective rooms. One huge trou-blesome third year had a habit of behaving badly and goad-ing the prefects by moving out of line and shouting when he could not be seen. This afternoon he was to try it out on me; when I pulled him up he brought all six foot four of himself against my relatively small build and height of five foot eight and threatened me, all the other third years shouting out, "Finish him off, Mitchell" and taking their encouragement he decided to head-butt me. In self-defence I instinctively defended myself and hit him in his mouth, which immediately split his lip and brought out blood. Seeing the blood on his shirt, the giant of a boy totally pan-icked and was like a lump of putty. The line got straight back in order and I marched him off to John Biginell, who asked me exactly what had happened. I explained in great detail, he then asked Mitchell for his version. Fortunately his version was exactly the same, he said, "I head-butted him and he punched me in the mouth." John Biginell asked him "What did you expect?" to which he replied "Look how I have come out."

After some time of discussion, Mitchell agreed that it was his fault and from that day Mitchell and I were friends, but many teachers called me aside and said, "Good two penny punch boy, if anyone deserved it he did." If a similar incident occurred in a school today there would have been a school inquiry and the rest. In my opinion, one of the problems of failing discipline in schools generally, is due to the lack of boundaries and all the help a perpetrator is given by the so called 'do-gooders' in society, I may not be politically correct but that is exactly what my view is

At the end of that academic year, I duly moved into the upper sixth form and also became one of eight senior prefects of the school, a privilege indeed as once a week we all sat on the stage with the select heads of departments and the Head of the School for assembly. School life could not have been better, recognition all round and obviously making great achievement in England

My last year at school was extremely eventful because we had made the grade in many ways, both David and I qualified for the Duke of Edinburgh's Award and we also had the special privilege of meeting Sir John Hunt of Everest fame on a personal basis, being invited to join Mrs Chetwynd and Major Biginell to have tea with Lord and Lady Hunt. Sir John had led the team that conquered Mount Everest with Sir Edmond Hilary and Sherpa Tensing. He personally went through my Duke of Edinburgh's expedition log book and asked me questions on how the expedition went, all very exciting for a second year in England and we were awarded the Silver Medal of the scheme. This achievement hit the newspapers in Ceylon with the headline *"Ceylon Boys Win Duke's Prize"*, and gave the story of the old Thomians, etc...

We both went on to carry out all the required sectors of the Gold Medal and anticipated a visit to Buckingham Palace, which was the practice then, for a personal presentation by Prince Philip. Sadly for me, although I completed all the sectors, I was refused the Gold Medal because I was a few weeks over the age limit, but David went on to get his and the Buckingham Palace meeting with Prince Philip The Duke of Edinburgh.

The final weeks of school meant A-level exams, which would determine how soon I could be articled at my place of work and the beginning of a chosen career within a professional environment. I had the whole summer holidays to spend gainfully before taking my position at Stoy Hayward.

During this short period, I took a part-time job in a restaurant called The Phoenix in Cavendish Square, just off Oxford Circus, washing dishes and being a kitchen assistant here. Once again I had a lesson in life which would serve me throughout my business career.

It happened on the second morning of my work at the restaurant, when the boss of the establishment asked me to clean both the Ladies and Gents lavatories before opening. I collected all the materials for the task and decided to do the cleaning of the Ladies room first. This I did very well because it was easy and ladies do not seem to make as much mess as the men. I then went to the Gents washroom which was a totally different ball game. To start with it was somewhat smelly and lots of splashes around. Feeling a little squeamish I did the job badly and I knew it. When I had finished, I was a little more than surprised that the restaurant boss came by to check my work. He could see instantly that I had not cleaned the Gent's urinals properly. He looked at me and without making a fuss simply said to me, "You obviously feel too important as a student to clean the lavatory properly so I had better do it myself." He hung up his jacket rolled up his sleeves and proceeded to clean the urinals properly. I stood by and watched uneasily and feeling quite ashamed of my poor effort and performance, when he finished he said "There, that is how it should be done." He rolled down his sleeves put his jacket on and left the lavatory.

I will never forget how humiliated and ashamed I felt about how he put my effort to shame and showed me by example how it should be done. I have used this example whenever any of my staff refused to do something properly. I simply take over the task. I have never needed to repeat it to the same person in all the years of my business life, all my subordinates have respected me for this and have followed my example; the ones that did not learn from this have not remained in the job for long afterwards. I think this was one of my best lessons in life and demonstrates the theory of 'lead by example' if one needs to do so.

It was not long before my time to start my training at Stoy Hayward and although I had months of anticipation and excitement, my first day brought me down to earth and reality with a huge bump – up to now I had spent the last two years in school as a sixth former, the deputy head boy and one of the select seniors at school and I had got used to being recognised by teachers and younger pupils alike and regarded as someone slightly special. In my mind, working at Stoy's was simply going to be an extension of this… Not so at all!

As I walked through the big doors and headed for the office, I was greeted by the receptionist shown into the basement, not at all plush like the visitors area. I was greeted by some-what grubby stairs and two large rooms filled with desks and several clerks sitting around. Nobody knew me and apart from a few friendly nods I was unrecognised, one hell of a shock. This was only made worse later that day when my boss, who was so friendly at my interview, only greeted me with a nod and a simple good morning, not what I expected at all. I had thought that Mr Langton was going to treat me as someone special, but why should he I was simply another trainee articled clerk. It took me some time to get used to this and make the transformation from school to the workplace.

The next few months passed by very quickly and I soon became one of the boys, not to be so is always a disaster. There were all the other trainee accountants, at various levels of their training, beginners like me, some intermedi-ates and others who were finalists, and of course the quali-fied seniors who were to be our guides and mentors. Apart from accountancy there was so much to learn about life and more to the point professional life in England.

Stoy Hayward was in my view a 'posh' firm because most of the other trainee articled clerks had come from wealthy homes and backgrounds and had got in to the firm mostly through parental and family connections – well I suppose in a way so had I through the Kenneth Hume and Edward Langton connection. Therefore, on reflection I think that this was where I picked up many of the skills that took me through to a higher level of business connections in England. At that time the English business establishment was fairly tight knit and breaking through this barrier was not simple, although my Burgher class oriented background and heritage also helped. The Burghers in my view were the ultimate class snobs in Ceylon, because they believed that they were somewhat superior to the others there. Either way this environment was the perfect grooming ground for my business ambitions.

There were a few people who were of particular importance and stood out to me more than the others. One such person was a guy whom I shall call Patrick as I wish him to anonymous, he who worked with me and was also younger than me; he was only nineteen at the time but had more confidence and front than many a tycoon. The first time I encountered him I thought he was one of the partners and not a second year articled clerk. He was a tall slim guy dressed in an impeccable three-piece suit with a red carnation in his button hole; when he entered the audit room he took everyone's attention and to this day I remember his first greeting, "Hello boys did you all have a good week end at the Hammersmith Palais, I was of course at the Establishment Club." He had the most natural way of putting everyone around him down without ever being rude.

Later on he also taught me the best lesson in standing up to others particularly in business; he had this most irritating habit of asking me to get him things in a most condescending manner. I remember quite well him saying, "Ian would you like to stretch your legs and get me a packet of fags." I always saw red but did it without any question for several weeks, although I detested doing so but did not know how to reply, until one day I simply said "No I don't... Why don't you stretch your own legs and get your own fags?" He never asked me again and I have never allowed anybody since then to treat me with indignity, whether in business or personal life. This has been one of the values that I have defended to this day, come what may. Several examples of the defence of my dignity follow in this story and I hope it will be something I impart to all my readers, as I have tried to impart to anyone I have trained in business.

Day to day work and training continued at Stoy's, as we used to call the firm, and quite soon I became known as one of the most reliable and hardworking trainee in my section with the expectation by my qualified seniors of a very high standard of work and knowledge in the tasks I used to undertake. My immediate boss at the time, Paul Hipps, later to become senior partner of the firm, quite liked my approach and ambition and told me that he expected me to achieve a place within the first 200 in the intermediate exams of the institute of chartered accountants, quite a compliment and expectation at the time, he even undertook to supervise my study papers and training program. Part of this keen interest may have been to promote his own career ambitions at the firm which were clearly noticeable to all other seniors and juniors alike. I always took note and great interest in the corporate games that ambitious individuals play in order to promote themselves and demolish the competing opposition, I found it exciting and interesting and I suppose I was pleased to learn how to play the game, which was to help me in my later business life.

3.

The Night that Changed My Life

It was Friday the 16th November and a very close school friend, with whom I had stayed in close touch, called at the door as he used to do several times a week and wanted my brother David and me to join him for a drive as he had just passed his driving test and wanted as much road practice as he could get. This was nothing unusual because it had happened before and after a few moments to check each other's movements both David and I decided to join him.

We set off from our home in Highbury to travel to Palmers Green, where David's girlfriend lived, once we got there we all went in and enjoyed a cup of coffee with her family and then decided to head back home. As we got back into the car David sat in the front passenger seat and announced that we should buy some chips on the way home. I sat in the back of the car. We duly stopped at the chip shop and as David and Dennis went into the shop, I quickly sat in the front passenger seat, much to David's annoyance when he returned to the car. We had a few words and I insisted on sitting in the front and after he gave in and got into the back we were back on our way home to Highbury, quite obviously fate played its hand and Dennis our friend ran into the back of a parked forty-ton tipper lorry that night.

I don't actually remember the accident or any part of it at all to this day; the first thing that I was aware of was the sound of ambulance bells – in the early sixties police cars and ambulances had a shrill bell as their siren – and some very confusing thoughts on and off at intervals, the sensation of a speeding vehicle and those bells of the ambulance again, all very vague and distant, which made no sense to me that anything that was happening, least of all to me, that is until I suddenly heard the voice of a woman holding my bandaged head and talking to me in a very broad Jamaican accent. At that moment I asked the lady where I was, she replied that I was at the Royal Northern Hospital Accident and Emergency department and that I had been involved in a serious car accident and that she was the nurse looking after me. I knew without any doubt that things did not seem good for me, because my whole face and head was covered in a bandage, except for an opening over my mouth, through which I could breathe. I feared the worst for my brother and Dennis the driver and immediately asked the lady what had happened to the others in the car, she replied that they were okay and that I had suffered the worst injuries in the crash.

I still remember very clearly that I was really worried that my mother or my aunt and uncle, with whom I lived, would not know what had happened to me and that I would die without being able to speak to any of them. I was also feeling extremely very cold and shivery throughout my entire body I also kept repeating that I was feeling cold, the nurse put another blanket over me and I must have drifted into unconsciousness again. The very next thing that I clearly remember was that someone was holding my hand and speaking to me saying Ian, this is Uncle Edward and I am here, how are you? I still also remember very clearly that I was filled with absolute sense of relief that finally my family knew that I had been involved in a serious car accident and what had happened to me. Almost immediately, I had a sense of relief that my family knew what had happened and were there, a great feeling of calm came over me, even though the last words I heard uttered by someone in the room before I fell asleep were "He is in God's hands now." I had lost all the feelings of being scared of dying.

The next thing I remember is waking up in a hospital ward surrounded by almost everyone I knew in London and many nursing staff checking all sorts of things like blood pressure, temperature, etc., all around me. I was truly surprised that I had so many visitors and only heard later that I was not expected to pull through and that I was on the danger list, because my palate was broken and could collapse at any time and there was nothing that could be done to stop that because if that happened, it would have resulted in a choking end. My family were told that the next seventy-two hours were critical and that every care was being taken to help me survive.

I discovered later on that the crash had happened on the Friday night and it was late on Saturday afternoon when I regained consciousness, after a four hour operation and eighty-two stitches in my nose. I had been split open all the way from the middle of my head to the back of my palate. The biggest post-operative problem was the stability of my palate holding out. There was nothing to do but hope and was the reason that so many people had come to the hospital, just in case I had not survived and made it through.

The doctors on duty over that weekend at the Royal Northern hospital were absolutely amazing; I will never forget them and their fight for my life. The house officer Dr Bell was at my bedside most of the weekend and the surgical registrar Mr Ivor Smith had assisted the consultant surgeon Mr Reginald Murley, who was called in for the operation, and then was on call for the weekend.

On the Sunday evening he saw me again, checked me out and left the ward for a few hours, but when I complained of a headache he came back from home within half an hour to check me out again. I was also very lucky with the consultant on call that weekend, Mr Reginald Murley of Harley Street fame and one of the best surgeons of the hospital had come in on the Saturday to perform the operations on me and another accident victim who was brought in on that day. All in all, the casualty sister must have been right when she said "He is in God's hands now."

The seventy-two hours duly passed and the medical team were pleased that I had survived, and some of the nurses were bringing in some of their colleagues showing them what a lot of good work the surgeons had done with my battered face. Needless to say I stayed in touch with both Mr Murley and Mr Smith for many years to come; Mr Smith went on to be a very successful and well known consultant vascular surgeon both at St Georges and at the Hammersmith Hospital.

As I recovered I became aware of many things about myself which I had not known previously and I learned how to cope with major setbacks. I was just three weeks away from my twenty-first birthday and the accident had all but destroyed my face and my looks for want of a better word. I had not looked at myself in a mirror I had no idea of the damage that had been caused, because the mind carries on the with the image of ones face as it was before, true enlightenment took place almost three weeks later when I looked in a mirror for the first time. I was horrified to say the least at what I saw. I had a huge red wound running from my forehead down to my mouth; I had two large wooden splints on either side of my nose and a wire going through the sides of my nose to hold the splints in place. There was also a hole about two centimetres wide and one centimetre deep in my forehead, in addition the front of my head was shaved and my forehead and my lips were hugely large and swollen and I had a blood-stained scar running from the centre of my head down to the right hand side of my lip, which was held together with stitches and pulled up on my face, Oh my God, to say I was shocked was the understatement of the year, I did not know whether to scream or cry, I simply stared at my face in the mirror for a while thinking about what I looked like and how I had been chatting and flirting with the nurses who had attended me for the past three weeks or so, not knowing what I looked like which was really quite ugly, like something out of a horror film.

I slowly walked back to my bed in the ward to gather my thoughts and ponder on what was to follow. As far as I knew apart from the injuries to my face there was relatively no other serious injuries to any vital organs and my eyes had been miraculously saved and as my cracked palate had held firm God must have looked after me throughout, that was my only explanation.

Now that I was back in the bed I realised why my girlfriend Penny at the time came to visit me the day after I regained consciousness and as soon as she reached my bedside she immediately fainted. Also my friend Dennis who was driving the car simply stood at my bedside crying, I felt so emotional and angry about both these events that I banned them both from visiting me.

Needless to say this car accident was going to change my life forever in many ways, but I had been lucky to survive, very lucky indeed…

I was duly told that I could leave hospital in a few days and that my consultant Mr Murley would see me as an out-patient to discuss any further plastic surgery options at a future date. I also recall a funny incident in that during all the time I was on the danger list, I was not afraid at all, but about two days before I left the hospital I saw the hospital vicar approach my bed and I flew into an immediate panic thinking that he was there and coming over to give me the last rites, the human mind is so strange.

Recovery from my car accident was slow in many ways and mentally painful mainly because I was at the beginning of my adult life and also because I had just embarked on the training and future career I was going to follow. Going back to work was going to be the next big test of character and guts because I was a young man, shy of my disfigurement and appearance, in a profession which required meeting people all the time, daily in fact. The office had been amazingly good about things and had told me to take whatever time I needed for recovery before I came back to work – the reality was that apart from my facial injuries thank God I was really okay and did not need to stay at home, in fact it would really be better for me to go back to work and get back to the reality of life after this setback.

I was now back at home recovering for a few weeks before deciding to go back to work, and I had to come to terms with my facial injuries and develop the mental strength to face the office and all my work mates. I was helped enormously by a few things going on in my life at the time. I had a great talking relationship with my uncle and aunt, with whom I lived and we shared a great sense of humour, and we were able to discuss my injuries quite openly and without any embarrassment. In addition, I had developed a few friendships with some of the student nurses on the ward who had looked after me and I used to phone them to chat for many months after the accident. One particular friendship developed over the months and I eventually got married to her a few years later.

I had agreed a date on which to return with my managers and was making preparations for the event, and I can recall with some amusement some of the hilarious events during this time. I had to laugh about them because it was a way to recover mentally and also come to terms with the situation. Needless to say there was a degree of preparation to my personal appearance which was necessary to mitigate the damage to my face. The first of which was to have a denture made to fill the gap where my front teeth had been knocked out by the impact of the car body to my face, so I saw a dentist who was both sympathetic with my case and very imaginative in his reconstruction effort. This comprised of a plate to my palate with two front teeth in the form of a temporary denture as no permanent repair could be contemplated for several months, due to swelling and healing of the injuries to my mouth. The denture was duly constructed and I have to say did its job in making my teeth look fine. In addition I had grown a moustache due to an inability to shave my upper lip as it had been severely cut and had quite a prominent scar on one side. The moustache did look quite becoming, except that where it was missing

34

where the scar was and I made a joke of it saying that it looked a bit moth-eaten, all my family laughed about it, but it helped me to face the public without embarrassment.

One of the funniest incidents took place on my first day back to work, that morning I arrived on the platform of the tube station at Highbury and Islington and was standing there waiting for the train. My next door neighbour passed me on the platform making a gesture towards his mouth which I thought was a little odd. I smiled as he passed by again doing the same thing and I thought he was behaving really strange, still not realising what he was trying to do. He passed by a third time grinning with one lip up and his finger pointing to his mouth, finally I realised that he was trying to tell me that I had forgotten my denture, having the situation of course I had to go back home to get my teeth before I went to the office.

Once in the office, I had all the managers and my work colleagues sympathising with the situation and telling me how lucky I was to be alive, it was really like a huge welcome party until one guy, Edwards by name, who could not handle the situation burst out saying "God if that had happened to me and my face looked like that I would never come to the office, I would have committed suicide." The entire room went silent and after a few seconds' people started telling me not to worry and that Edwards simply could not handle the sight of a semi healed injury, the truth for me was that it made me feel strong and confident. Thank God!

4.

The Reality of Life After the Accident

Among all my friends and acquaintances there were different reactions, some pleasant and supportive and others simply shock and horror. In fact one evening I got on a bus with my brother and we recognised a friend who was already on the bus, we greeted him as usual when he turned toward me and said do I know you? When I told him who I was he simply said that he was sorry and he had not recognised my face. Whatever the reaction of those who knew me before, I believe that it gave me an inner strength which proved to be useful in my later life, particularly in business. One other hidden benefit that seemed to surface was that my broken nose gave me a tough bruiser-like look which was a lot different to the somewhat sharp features that I had before the crash.

Life at the office and at home was gradually returning to normal despite the after-effects of the accident and the normal fallout of such an incident, which is quite unpredictable at the time but takes its toll in many different ways. My girlfriend at the time of the crash who had visited me in the hospital and fainted at my bedside, which was quite a dramatic moment at the time, but I clearly remember how irritated it made me feel especially as I had asked her not to visit again, not quite sure why I suppose it was because I did not want her to feel sorry for me. It was something I have hated to this day, needless to say the friendship fizzled out after a few months and we lost touch completely over the next few years. My family had grown somewhat closer to me and I had also started new friendships both in the office and with some of the people I met in the hospital, this started a new chapter in the social side of my life, partly I suppose because they were more comfortable with my facial injuries. I never really tried to analyse these at the time, but it may have been because I was reluctant to see friends from the past.

I understood later from my father who still lived in Ceylon that many of my friends and relations had been shocked and horrified at the sequence of events in London and the accident together with my life-threatening injuries.

During the time of my recovery, one evening I was speaking with a doctor friend of mine Michael who was visiting England to take his FRCS exam, and was in social contact with me at the time of the accident. He had noticed that I kept using my handkerchief on my nose a lot of the time and asked why I did it so frequently, I told him that my nose was always running since the accident and he inquired what colour of the fluid was to which I replied quite clear. He immediately asked me to get ready and took me straight the Royal Northern Hospital, without giving me any reasons whatsoever, simply saying that it was better to have it checked out. Michael went to the admittance counter and spoke to the people there and after a few minutes I was taken into see a doctor who introduced himself as Mr Mullins the neurosurgical surgeon and the registrar on duty at the time. This all happened in the Accident and Emergency unit which in those days was the casualty department.

Many more detailed examinations followed and Michael was chatting in great detail to Mr Mullins, who then informed me that they thought it better to admit me into the neurosurgical unit for observation. Somewhat alarmed I inquired why this was so sudden and why it was necessary. I was told that the fluid running out of my nose could have been cerebral spinal fluid (CSF) from a possible hairline fracture in the base of my skull and I needed to have this checked out more thoroughly and seen by the consultant the next day.

I spent the night back in hospital and was seen by Mr Oliver the neurological consultant the very next day. After an initial examination he turned to his registrar, Mr Mullins and I heard him tell a story that chilled me, which was about a previous patient of his who had similar symptoms and ended up contracting meningitis through the hairline fracture. He said we are not going to take any chances until we are sure it is safe to let him out. Michael was absolutely right to bring me in to A&E when he did. It also showed why he ended up being one of the leading and most dedicated surgeons Ceylon ever had.

After the consultation with the neurosurgical consultant I was given a little clear sterile bottle to collect any discharge from my nostril and this was analysed over the next three to five days, and I was seen again by the neurosurgical team. The good news was that all the tests were negative and I was going to be allowed out, but with a proviso which was that I carried a little bottle and a card in my wallet asking that I be admitted to Mr Oliver's ward as an emergency if ever needed. I also had to visit his clinic once a week for the next few months, which then changed to once a month, this carried on for several years during which time I became friends with Mr Mullins, until I stopped being monitored for CSF. Something to remember well is that all in all the NHS had served me brilliantly ever since my accident and I have the utmost respect for all the doctors and staff who helped me recover. The overriding fact was that I was simply a young boy who was scraped off the road by an ambulance team and brought into an A&E department, one Friday night, but had all the attention of some of the finest doctors who attended me all on the world famous NHS.

I also found out that my father in Ceylon was not informed of the accident and my condition at the time of the car crash or for several days, until I was off the critical list, in case I had not made it. In view of my survival and subsequent recovery it was several months before my father visited me in London to see for himself the results.

5.

The Early Days in Ceylon

My parents had divorced when I was only about four years old and my brother David and I had lived most of our childhood lives on a shared basis between my mother and father and there was a huge amount of acrimony between both parties, and especially my fathers' family, who thought that my mother was to blame for the family break-up. They all extracted every bit of revenge on my mother and indirectly on any part of her family that they could affect; this was especially done by my paternal grandfather Charlie Anthonisz.

I have a very clear recollection of Charlie and he always had a sadistic streak about him. He was a surveyor by profession and was very old school in his demeanour with a zero tolerance on almost everything to do with his own wider family and us. After my parents' divorce, my father won the custody battle and David and I were brought to live with my grandparents at what was the 'family compound', which was a very large house with several parts to it. The house was occupied by my paternal grandparents and my fathers' sisters, together with their respective families, a little bit like the South Fork Ranch in the TV *Dallas* series, although I must add immediately, not on anywhere the same scale of wealth and luxury. It was not uncommon in the day for this to be the case in Colonial Ceylon.

Under the communal living setup of my aunts and my cousins, each family had their parents to safeguard and protect them from the direct control of my grandfather. Unfortunately however, my dad was somewhat weak as an individual and seemed particularly so after what was a very messy and highly controversial divorce. He was therefore very dependent on his parents and this resulted in David and I being under the direct supervision of my grandfather Charlie.

Whatever his motives were, he was a particularly nasty piece of work and an unquestionable bully. I have no doubt that this influence on my early childhood has always made me stand up to a bully whatever his size and strength and has helped me to take a very tough stance against any bully I have come across in my life, and has driven me to assist any person I feel is being bullied by an individual or an organisation. It has made me to stand up for what I believed in since I was old enough to do so and in my entire adult life.

Although there were so many instances I could relate about Charlie, I would like to recall just a few to give and idea of what David and I went through as young children. One of the earliest I recall of Charlie's nasty manoeuvres soon after the divorce was to deliberately delay us when my mother arrived to pick us up on the weekend. He would make my mother wait outside the house for a very long time while we were getting ready to leave. As we were quite young and dependant on the adults in the setup, he would ask the servants to slow down the process and take as long as possible to get us ready. Naturally this upset us as very young children and invariably my mother would suspect his little game, which resulted in a weekly confrontation between my mother and my paternal family, something that made David and I despise Charlie and some other members of the family.

Charlie also used to beat us with a cane for almost anything we did wrong, in fact it got to a stage when he used to use six canes; three in each hand, the offences is included school performance and reports or simple domestic situations such as getting home late from school or any minor disobedience of any degree.

The beatings and canings got worse as we grew older and our feelings toward him were a mixture of fear and hate. All this time my father was aware of the way Charlie treated us but his interpretation of the situation was that Charlie loved us and behaved like this for our own good and benefit. I personally think that it was his inability to confront his father because it could have resulted in him having to leave my grandparents' house or have to return us to my mother's custody, neither of which he wanted to do.

The final straw came when we were around twelve or thirteen years old were in the process of receiving one of those beatings, David grabbed one of the sets of canes off our grandfather Charlie and turned the tables by using them on him. He was so shocked at David's response that he stopped in his tracks and withdrew from the situation. This was an entirely new scenario for both parties, Charlie on the one hand and David and me on the other. My recollection of events thereafter was that soon after the incident Charlie had to undergo some cardiac-related medical tests, which was followed by a period of some weeks in hospital and was visited by many members of the family. I do not recall seeing him return from the hospital and my recollection is that he never returned home alive.

I feel that this part of our childhood made both David and I very independent and strong in relation to how we behaved to others. As brothers, although we may have with fought with each we always stood together back to back against the rest of the world.

Growing up in Ceylon was a rich experience in its entirety; both David and I were pupils at St Thomas' College a boy's public school in the English tradition and based on Winchester College in Hampshire. The College and was over a hundred years old, my grandfather and my father were also pupils there, and the College and family tradition came together in this institution. In Ceylon, being a Thomian, namely a pupil or former pupil of St Thomas' was in itself like a qualification and like a gateway to a better life, for most of its pupils it was recognition in itself. It is not something that is easily explained and can only be paralleled with like having been to Eton in the UK.

As I have said before pupils at St Thomas' were a varied mix very rich, middle class and some poorer, but what we all had in common which was that we were all Thomians and this gave us all equal status with the best. Being a member of the first eleven cricket team was considered to be better that having A-levels.

Our school motto **"Esto Perpetua"** was ingrained into our very being, 'Be Thou Forever'... in English

One of its famous headmasters wrote:

"You belong to one of the best schools in the world, a school with splendid traditions and the most honourable name and I charge you to try and hand down those traditions and that name untarnished and unimpaired."

With this background, it is therefore, not surprising that David and I were easily able to get on in the UK our new home and of course, we had this inner confidence with us wherever we went.

Apart from the heritage of this school, the social exposure of being classmates with the sons of some of the richest and most powerful in the land, together the sons of simple ordinary people, gave one a sense of equality with the rich and poor alike and I have always been equally at ease in my business life with all types of people, those who were very successful, together with some of the most ordinary folk and have always been able to communicate at each individual level. I attribute this to my schooling and the heritage of St Thomas' College.

The attached illustrations give an idea of what St Thomas' College was like and why it played such an important part of our lives and upbringing, including the traditions which all Thomians followed. The main buildings of the school were built on the four sides of a large quadrangle. The College Chapel – 'The Chapel of the Transfiguration' was at the highest point and the Physics and Chemistry laboratories opposite. Likewise, the Assembly hall and the main classroom block were on the other two sides and faced each other.

In all this was an awe-inspiring and magnificent sight particularly when revisited after some years as a past pupil, I have visited many times and taken many of my British friends to visit, every single one has been very impressed.

Assembly Hall – **Picture Courtesy Peter Nicol**

College Chapel & Quadrangle – **Picture Courtesy Peter Nicol**

Class Room Buildings & Quadrangle –
Picture Courtesy of Peter Nicol

Science Laboratories & Quadrangle –
Picture Courtesy of Peter Nicol

College Crest & Motto

Altar of School Chapel – **Picture Courtesy of Peter Nicol**

In addition to the buildings of the school, its location was by the sea, boasting one of the prettiest bays in Colombo called Mount Lavinia.

Mount Lavinia bay – **Picture Courtesy Peter Nicol**

This was the beach which most of the Colombo folk used to come to swim at on a Sunday morning and was adjoining St Thomas' College

Our childhood in Ceylon was an exciting an eventful adventure for both David and me and we had many opportunities to visit various parts of the island throughout our childhood years in Ceylon. My uncle Edward, my father's elder brother, was the headmaster for government schools: Teachers at that time were highly respected members of the community like doctors, lawyers and accountants, especially in Ceylon, where the entire community treated them as being learned persons, particularly the position of a school headmaster.

Uncle Edward had been appointed to several schools particularly when there was a need to rectify an existing problem or to put right a weakness that existed locally; most times he became involved in the local community and was friends with local leaders, such as the village headman and the local chief of police.

During these appointments and during the school holidays when the school was closed, Uncle Edward would round up all our cousins and sometimes their parents and take us to his house at the school. Most of our visits to parts of the hill country one place called Passara were during a such posting and an even longer posting he had was in the south of the Island, a place called Weeraketiya near where the recent President Mahinda Rajapaksa comes, they were totally diverse parts of the island.

The hill country was on the one hand, which was where the tea was grown in beautifully groomed plantations with precise cultivation and well cared for roads; everything was neatly trimmed and pretty. I always thought of this part of the island like a tropical Switzerland. There was also a presence of many European planters, mainly Scottish and English, who had established themselves in Ceylon for many years from when they first arrived some 150 years earlier; in many ways it was like a mini-England.

Hill Country Tea Plantation – **Picture courtesy of Bob Dobbs**

Typical Waterfall (1) – **Picture Courtesy of Peter Nicol**

We also participated in very local life styles such as bathing under the waterfalls from the high mountains, which was an experience not to be forgotten; the water was freezing cold but had to be experienced for one to really appreciate this wonder of nature; we all did many times and have to say that it was an unparalleled experience.

Typical Waterfall (2) – **Picture Courtesy of Peter Nicol**

In contrast the south-east of the island was dry and wild in terms of terrain vegetation. Although we were young, we were old enough to appreciate the difference, and although we did not know it at the time we were being educated about the environment and how life went on far outside the capital city, Colombo.

Each school holiday we would spend many weeks in this environment and were exposed to meet local businessmen and politicians of varying stature, as they were local social contacts of my uncle Edward who as I have mentioned was the headmaster of the large government central school in a place called Weeraketiya of course in those days a headmaster was a highly respected member of the local community as was the local MP the area Superindent of police and individuals of similar standing. Being in this position we were invited to join these people and their families for meals, parties and even wild game hunting. We learned how to use a double barrelled shotgun, how hunt wild boar and how to observe leopards and even elephants, all of this had discipline and strict rules. Our exposure to nature and wildlife was unparalleled compared to youngsters who grew up in highly developed countries or cities as we saw life somewhat in the raw.

Dry Zone Jungle – **Picture Courtesy of Peter Nicol**

Elephants feeding in the jungle – **Picture courtesy of Peter Nicol**

Wild Peacock in the Jungle – **Picture Courtesy of Peter Nicol**

In order to conserve water in the dry zone there were man-made lakes known as 'tanks' which were in fact large reservoirs for irrigation of fields and for use by the villagers and local communities for all their needs such as bathing, fishing, washing clothes and a source of water. David and together with our cousins went fishing and swimming in the tank on many occasions after which we would fry the fish we had just caught for a hearty meal

Tank at Walasmulla – **Picture courtesy of Peter Nicol**

Looking back now, I realise that the richness of our early teen years and these experiences gave us a very different perspective to children who grew up in big cities and may have had a lot to do in my approach to life in general and my approach to business and self-reliance.

My family being what would be described as middle class and therefore had, which followed in Ceylon at that time, the privilege of having domestic house staff in a normal family set-up. It was quite usual in our homes to have a complement of a cook, a housemaid and a houseboy. Growing up in a set-up of this kind gave me an expectation that I could delegate work to the staff and it would be carried out, something which came to me very easily later on when I was a manager and eventually ran my own businesses. Of course, the manner in which one delegated and the expectation as to how it was carried out was quite individual to different members of the family. I always found that I was able to request and get the best quality of service and from all our house staff. I even managed to cultivate staff loyalty at the relative young age of around eleven or twelve. I say this because I clearly remember an incident when my mother had a confrontation with one of the houseboys, who retorted quite cheekily that he would work for Mr Ian when I grew up – needless to say the boy got the sack for his cheek and I was in the doghouse for several days for "encouraging the servants" as it was put to me. I was secretly very pleased to know that anything the houseboy had done for me was done because he respected me and had appreciated how I treated him, obviously I had cultivated had a degree of devotion of duty in him. I recall that after our move to the UK many of the house staff kept in touch with me for a considerable time, particularly as they managed to write to me in English with news updates on their personal lives and changing fortunes, something I greatly appreciated.

Living and growing up in Colombo gave me some of the best experiences in my adolescent years. In world terms it was a small city and most professional and middle class families had knew or heard of each other because it was a relatively small social circle. Of course the contrast of richer and poorer existed in the background, particularly in an institution such as St Thomas' College.

Most young boys including David and me had bicycles on which we went to school and socialised with our friends after school. I would also like to recall how I came by the possession of the best bicycle in the country. A close, well-off schoolmate of mine, possibly one of my closest friends, had an exclusive bicycle sent to him from England. It was a Hercules Tour de France, a magnificent machine, metallic maroon in colour with every available gizmo of the time making it an unmistakable sight on the Colombo roads, whenever it was ridden by the owner. About six months after he acquired it, his parents decided to send him to the UK to finish his studies and of course, the maroon fantasy was put up for sale, needless to say the price was way beyond most of our reaches. However a very rich friend in our circle said he would buy it, but could not take it home because he was not allowed to ride a bike on the streets. During this conversation, I instinctively offered to keep it for him and ride it to school daily for him to enjoy it whenever he wanted to. He agreed and without any hesitation bought the bike and gave it to me to take home and use as my own, with the proviso that I allowed him a ride whenever possible – why would I not agree?

In an instant, I possessed what was the most desired bicycle among any cycle enthusiast in the country. I enjoyed the prestige, admiration and in some case the envy of so many youngsters around. Whenever I stopped anywhere, many boys sometimes girls gathered to talk to me about 'my bike' it was quite something to take in especially since I had not paid a penny (or cent) for it, this made it even more enjoyable.

There was however a disappointing end to the story after about a year, it appeared that my friend shared his secret with his chauffer who duly reported the facts to his parents and alas, they turned up in their huge family car, put the bicycle in the boot and drove off, leaving me feeling so sorry for myself and having to get back to the normal world. However, I did enjoy everything relating to it while it lasted, and felt that I had the amazing good fortune to have this bike as my own for so long, through nothing more than the luck of life, or making a quick on the spot decision for which I have always been truly grateful.

I need to mention that this was not the first time good fortune had played a part in my ambitions to acquire things that all young boys dream of. My first camera was given to me by an aunt who saw me admiring her camera as she was packing it for a holiday in India and I suppose my interest in it was so intense that she simply said would you like to have it. My reaction was but it is yours and she simply responded that she would buy a new one in India, so I was the proud owner of a camera, instantly.

My first watch was acquired through an even funnier episode when my brother David had just been given a watch with a see-through back to it by an uncle. I noticed that there was a role of cellotape lying beside it. I asked my uncle if I may have the cellotape he said yes! Suddenly, for some reason David preferred to have the roll of tape and immediately exchanged it with me for the watch, to this day I cannot imagine why and can only assume that different things appeal to different people, thus I had my first watch. I relate these events to record the fact that life is full of opportunity and some of us see it seize the moment, others see it and do nothing about it much has been said about people being lucky, I am not sure how it works but I am aware that successful people are those who see and opportunity and take it, rather than simply talk about it.

My sense of respect for behaviour in society and established customs must have been instilled in me from my early life at St Thomas' and my parents as members of the Burgher community where the values of honesty, integrity and loyalty were paramount and where behaving like a gentleman and treating others with respect was the norm. Sadly, it seems that in many countries nowadays, these values have been replaced by a lack of moral integrity and the idea making a quick buck by whatever means prevails. Fortunately, I have found that what some people refer to old-fashioned values still exist among some of us.

During my education at St Thomas', the authority of the head and the loyalty to the school and the 'college flag' was unquestionable; this coupled with the values the Burgher society in Ceylon adopted, were what was referred by some as the old English values. These were passed on to each younger generation as would have been the normal society life and was how I was brought up. I have always considered this factor to have helped me to integrate into British society easily and to help me develop my business and social life in the United Kingdom.

6.

The Move to England

It was amidst this lifestyle and juncture in our lives that my mother decided to consider leaving the sunny Ceylon to seek a new life in England. The background was not entirely surprising because in 1958 the country experienced the first full scale race riot in over forty years; these events shattered the trust the Sinhalese majority and the Tamil minority communities had in one another, which in turn led to further polarisation. This coupled with the act in 1956 to make Sinhala the official language of the country in place English was the beginning of the well-known mass emigration of the Burgher and Tamil communities from Ceylon to countries such as England, Australia, Canada and the US.

There was a general feeling among the Burgher and Tamil communities at that time that unless you were Sinhalese opportunities would not be as good, and that favouritism would creep in for jobs and promotions in the future, particularly as the first language had now been changed to Sinhala instead of English and the result of this being having to learn Sinhala to a much higher level as a first language. This did not sit well with the Burgher community at large. The talk of migration to an English speaking country such as the United Kingdom and Australia had begun. It is well documented that by the mid-sixties and seventies large numbers of the burgher communities had left for the UK and more so to Australia. In 1973 when the Australian government ended the Australian, all white immigration policy these numbers increased dramatically.

In our particular case, my stepfather was Tamil – together with being a government employee, being overlooked for future promotion stared him in the face. There was an air of despondency at large. My mother took the decision to move to the UK, she sought permission from my father to take David, and me with her. My father thought that it was an opportunity for us especially as I had a paternal uncle in London and so the die was cast for this huge change.

The preparation for this trip was one of mixed feelings; on the one hand, it was the move to a new country, which many have dreamed of particularly as it was England, which was portrayed as the motherland of the empire and London, where it all happened and we as Ceylonese only read about! In addition, there the dimensions of adventure that made us somewhat different to our contemporaries in Ceylon who did not have this opportunity, and this made us as a family feel quite special and privileged

On the other hand leaving St Thomas' college our beloved institution, our school and other friends and most of all in David's and my case leaving our father behind in Ceylon permanently. I can only describe as the feeling of excitement tinged with sadness.

Our scheduled departure from Colombo the 16th of July and we would reach London on the 3rd of August, so there was a sea voyage of eighteen days on a luxury liner to look forward to and get excited about. The whole idea of this was quite overwhelming because one had to prepare for it, especially as it was the days of formal wear for a voyage, and both David and I had to be kitted out for the occasion of a send-off. We both had a new suit each and travel bags; this was indeed very special and exciting. I imagine it would have left all our cousins somewhat envious at the time.

In the early sixties the normal mode of travel was by ship and only very rich and privileged travellers travelled by air and it too took several days with many refuelling stops. Apart from which, moving countries entailed having huge amounts of luggage to take all one's possessions to the new country; we both had huge cabin trunks for this purpose.

The day of travel duly arrived and the "**SS *Orsova***" which was the largest liner belonging to the P&O line which could go through the Red Sea at the time. It carried almost 1,500 passengers and weighed 33,000 tons. The ship was due to weigh anchor at midnight. In the day, this was quite a special event because ships had to be escorted out of the harbour by two tugboats amid the sound of foghorns of the other ships in port and of the departing ship itself.

The farewell on the quayside to all our friends and relations who had gathered for the occasion was excitement tinged with sadness, with wonder if we would ever meet again, certainly some of us would not; especially the older uncles and aunts. In my case, it would be over twenty-two years before I visited Ceylon, now Sri Lanka, again.

We boarded the vessel which was to be our home for the next eighteen days and got settled in our cabins, we then headed for the decks to watch it leave the harbour amid the sounds of the foghorns and watch the shore fade into the distance as we started the six-day crossing to the African continent.

The liner was en-route to London via Colombo where it had stopped for supplies and passengers and had many ex-European immigrants heading back 'home' for a visit to their homelands and relatives left behind. David and I shared a dining table with such a couple, Carol and Bill, who explained that they were returning to visit England after living in Australia for ten years; it was from them that I learned that the Australians referred to English people as 'Poms'.

Although the days of cruises as holidays had not arrived, overseas travel by ship was still quite an experience and the idea of having all one's meals, treats and entertainment provided as part of the fare was all very new to us and was something to enjoy and savour. In any case it was going to be a 'once in a lifetime' experience, this we did my brother David was just over a year younger that me and enjoyed all this as much as I did. My youngest brother Darrell was over eight years younger than David and me and may not have had the same experience but I am sure enjoyed the adventure in his own way.

The entertainment on board the *Orsova* was quite something. I would say even extraordinary, something different every night and organised events on a daily basis, and our friendship with our table companions Carol and Bill was an education on what to expect in England. They always had plenty of tips and information to pass on. I am sure they did come in use during our first weeks and months in England.

I cannot miss the story of the 'deck quoits' championship of our voyage which was announced over the ship's speaker system while we having breakfast one morning. Needless to say I had no idea what deck quoits was, but Carol told us that we would enjoy it and urged David and me to enter the competition and take part. We both told them that we had no idea how to play and Bill told us that he would teach us the game.

Deck quoits is a game played on the deck of a ship in which rope ring is aimed at a target painted on the deck and played commonly on cruise ships, and each player would normally have either three or four of them. The object of the game is to get most of your quoits on the centre of the target, very similar to bowls. The areas between each circle are marked with their scoring amounts. The outer rings score less than the inner rings.

Immediately after breakfast, we were all up on the deck having tuition and practice on the game of deck quoits from our friend Bill and we were soon to get the hang of it.

Not long after the commencement of the championship was announced. Being a large ship there was a large number of entrants; many doing it simply for the fun of it and soon only the serious contestants were left. David and I were among these because our school St Thomas' was a very competitive sports school and we brought up that way. Carol announced that Bill would probably win the game because he had won the championship on the ship between Australia and Ceylon; in any case, he was our mentor.

It so happened, that Bill beat all his opposition and so did I, only to find that I would face my coach and mentor Bill in the final, this was exciting indeed. It was a neck and neck game until Bill had thrown the final ring and it was sitting on the centre of the target, it was now my turn, with my final quoit and I had to knock his out of the target to win. I had a brilliant teacher and without sounding too arrogant, I did this in great style to win the championship from my mentor. It was all a big laugh but astounded both Bill and Carol and was the talk of our dining table for many days to come.

After six days of cruising across the Indian Ocean, we reached the port of Aden; this is a very important, recognised by the world port, and lies directly on all major international shipping routes. It is also a very special port being one of the five best natural harbours in the world. The crossing from Ceylon to the northwest of Africa was somewhat choppy and David was unable to eat for a few days due to seasickness, and sometimes playing table tennis was difficult as the ball disappeared from the bat but it was all part of the experience and in my mind was to be enjoyed.

Aden was our first port of call and was a duty-free port and was great for shopping and that was what we all did. In addition, the challenge was the intense bargaining with the Arab traders and I am sure we all thought we had won the day. After we returned to the ship, the dinner conversation was all about what we bought and at what price.

When my mother had announced that we were going to England in a few months I had planned to buy a folding camera, realised my dream, and was showing off my purchase to everyone, I still have it today and reminisce on the voyage and Aden whenever I see it.

The crossing of the Red Sea was the next part of the voyage and of course, at the end of the Red Sea was the Suez Canal. It was something we had read about, particularly as it was soon after the political crisis when Egypt nationalised the canal. The Orsova was the largest liner to be able to go through it at the time and it took a whole day to accomplish, most of the passengers stood on deck watching the banks of the canal as it slowly passed through under the control of a special pilot.

The next port of call was at the other end of the Suez Canal, it was Port Said, a port that lies at the north end of the Suez Canal and lies in northeast of the Mediterranean coast. The city was established in 1859 during the building of the Suez Canal. It was also a fuelling station for ships that pass through the Suez Canal. It thrives on being a duty-free port and it is home to the lighthouse of Port Said which was the first building in the world built from reinforced concrete. Needless to say we disembarked here too and enjoyed the shopping, all an exciting new experience to our entire family on the ship. Once through the Suez our voyage was mainly dropping off returning migrants and refuelling and restocking stops for the ships supplies, we called at the Italian port Naples, then the French port of Marseilles, and Gibraltar at the tip of Spain. The voyage through all these places ended up in shopping and more shopping until we finally went through to the Bay of Biscay to dock at Tilbury in England and our anticipated new life in England.

7.

Moving on Professionally

I had completed my contract with Stoy Hayward. I had now been with them for around six years, and although I had been out of contract for a few months, I had not had a review of my contract salary. Therefore, I decided that it was time to find out whether I had a more permanent and fruitful future with the company where I had trained or if I had to seek promotion and a higher salary elsewhere. I therefore decided to grab the bull by the horns and have a chat with my departmental partner, who was one of the more senior partners of the firm and having made the necessary arrangements with his secretary went into his office to discuss the matter.

Our meeting started with the usual niceties about how I was doing and whether I enjoyed working there, which I answered very positively, but then we soon we got down to the crux of the meeting when I told him that I was doing seniors' work and that as I was out of contract. I also thought that I deserved a salary review. He looked at me squarely as though I had dropped a bombshell and immediately said, "Anthonisz, I don't need you to come in here to tell me how good and valuable you are to the firm, I have ways of finding that out myself, get out of my office now…"

Although I was a little shocked at his response, I left his office determinedly and decided instantly that I was going to look for a job elsewhere. My mind went into overdrive and I remembered that a previous manager whom I had worked with at Stoy's, Michael by name, who had recently joined another up and coming firm close by in the West End of London and was a partner designate there. I phoned Michael told him my story and asked if his new firm had any vacancies in their audit department. Michael replied that he thought there might be and that he would come back to me.

Within two hours of my phone call to Michael, I had made an interview appointment with one of the partners of Blick Rothenberg for the next day. Once again, the network of whom you know rather than what had worked in my favour, in a few hours.

The interview itself was almost a mere formality because Bob Glatter, my new boss to be, had found out everything he wanted to know about me from Michael and simply said Michael has recommended you very highly and I could use you on my team, when will you be free to join us? I was reeling with delight and excitement. I had a job with a smaller but equally respected firm at a really decent salary and a promotion to the status of an audit senior at almost 50% more than what I was getting after my contract. I skipped back to the office with excitement.

Leaving Stoy's was an emotional experience, because I was happy there and had made many professional friends and connections and most of all had learned a huge amount about accountancy and business. It was also the employer that saw me through the difficult days after my accident and the long recovery process that followed, but in life I have always thought that life is a two-way street, one gets back what one puts into the game and I gave my employer my best all the time that I was there.

I am pleased to say that all my managers and the partners seemed genuinely sorry to see me leave. However, the reality of the situation was that it is much harder to progress in a firm where you had been a junior and had been trained there, because as long you are perceived as being a junior or a trainee it takes a lot longer to be recognised. This rule does not apply of course if one had the social connections at the highest level, in which this case didn't apply. Certainly, this was my analysis of the situation.

At that time Blick Rothenberg was roughly half the size of Stoy Hayward and starting at Blick's was to me like a breath of fresh air. I started there as a senior and was introduced as such to everyone whom I met. My first assignment was to run one of Bob's largest audits as one of his seniors in charge, because his actual manager was away on an extended holiday. This gave me the opportunity to show if I could rise to the occasion.

I did not have long to wait because my assistant on the job was a very capable, clever articled clerk who in addition to his capabilities had a disobedient streak and wanted to get his own way if at all possible. I had been warned about this by my boss Bob. On the second day of the job, I asked him to carry out a specific task and he wanted to know why he had to do that, in addition he thought that he knew a better way to get the result. I insisted that he did it my way and he wanted me to justify to him as to why he had to do it. I realised that not only did I have to establish myself as the senior on the job, but I needed to feel confident enough to run the job my way, otherwise I would have been finished both as his junior and my own confidence would have been dented on my first job with a new employer.

I faced the situation by giving my colleague a simple choice, either do what I asked you to do my way or go back to the office on his own, as I did not need him anymore. He was taken by total surprise; his reply was "What shall I tell them when I get there?" I said, "Just tell them that Ian does not need you anymore and I will explain the problem to our mutual boss." He stayed and did it my way; thereafter we worked as a great team for many years and remain great personal friends to this day. The business and management lesson to be learned from this type of situation was that you must stand your ground when you are right and challenged, otherwise you will lose respect especially from your juniors and subordinates.

It is also my view this is one of the reasons that bosses find it difficult to establish their authority and breed the climate of weak management which seems to dominate the workplace today. This was only the beginning of my successful stay at Blick's and my fruitful working relationship with Bob Glatter.

Blick's was an exciting place for me simply because I had come from Stoy's, a bigger and much more prestigious firm and my boss, together with my other colleagues treated me with a degree of respect and knowledge that I had not been accustomed to, this was a great experience and needless to say I made the most of it, imparting any knowledge I had and any advanced practice that had been carried out at Stoy's during my stay there.

One particular special event that I recall was the use of permanent audit files, something which has been common practice now for several decades. At that time, Blick's had not begun the practice and I told my Bob Glatter that we had used them at Stoy's and while my conversation was going on the senior partner of Blick's walked in. Much to my surprise Bob Glatter included him in the conversation and told him what we were talking about – almost immediately I was given the task of introducing them at Blick's. I was flattered and excited at the thought of being in charge of the exercise and was charged with organising the staff to do some paid overtime over the next few weekends to complete it.

At the end of the task all the helpers were duly paid their overtime dues, and when I put in my claim Bob told me that I was not due any because I had been in charge of the project and that my reward would come at my next review. I was both surprised and gutted not to get immediate recognition of my brainwave… Welcome to the management!

I must add that I was certainly well-rewarded financially when my review came. In addition what I had done was recognised and remembered for several years, so much so that when both my sons joined Blick Rothenberg for their training as chartered accountants many years later, they were told by some of the people that were acquainted with me during my stay there, "Your father instituted the permanent audit file system here." I was flattered and enjoyed the fact that this had been remembered by more than my immediate colleagues. It is also a lesson for any young ambitious person to be bold enough to come forward with ideas, however simple they think it may be, all too often people are reluctant to show their light for fear of rejection, or embarrassment, my advice is "Be bold enough to go for it."

My position at Blick's improved throughout my stay there. This enabled me to gain invaluable experience at the highest end of professional accounting mainly because of the constant interaction at managers' and partners' levels and soon I had an opportunity trust into my lap to become a manager myself. Although I had direct contact with Bob Glatter, the partner whose team I worked with, I did have an immediate manager with whom I worked on a day-to-day basis. My opportunity came when suddenly my manager broke his arm somewhat badly and was out of action for several months, initially I was brought in to deputise him and supervise the two teams he was in charge of, and subsequently I was given the job permanently. Although my break was largely due to luck, my advice to any up and coming employee or entrepreneur is once again is to seize every opportunity you get. I have often thought that the difference between someone who is successful and someone who is not is that the successful one sees and opportunity and takes it while the other sees it and simply thinks about it…

As the firm grew, I was lucky enough to grow with them and as the internal organisation became more structured, I was able to carve out a position within the growth and establish myself in all aspects of a professional firm. I have always cherished leadership and all that goes with it, therefore I always volunteered for any extra roles that were offered and made sure I delivered; I always worked on time deadline jobs, and was willing to work late whenever necessary. My efforts were always recognised by the partners of the firm and I was always ready to think about any possible improvements to any of the existing systems and offer them to the partners.

It is with some degree of humility that I must say that I became a valued and respected member of the senior staff of the firm and in absolute fairness to them the financial recognition was always forth coming from the firm. I can sincerely say that my stay at Blick Rothenberg was both rewarding and extremely successful from both an experience and financial perspective.

Being a first-generation immigrant, I have been asked the question many times if I had experienced racial discrimination in England, and on each occasion this has come as a bit of a surprise to me, mainly because I have never consciously thought of myself as being different and, having thought about it carefully, I can say that I have experienced some kind of discrimination on just one single occasion. This happened when I was attending a new audit as the second in command, we arrived at the clients and my boss introduced me and the junior clerk to the managing director and we settled in to the room. A few minutes later my boss was invited for coffee by the MD on his own, I thought nothing of it at the time but over the next few days noticed that he never spoke directly to me and always communicated with me through his deputy.

My boss was recalled to the office, I was left in charge of the job, and it became a little more obvious that there was a little discomfort between me and the MD of the company which I could not put a reason to. A week later, I had finished the accounts and approached him to ask for a meeting to discuss the results to which he responded by saying he would see my boss about the results, but he paused for a moment and asked how the company had done. When I told him that they had made a loss he went absolutely mad, told me I was wrong and immediately invited me in to his office to check my figures and tell me where I had made a mistake, we checked everything thoroughly but he could not find anything wrong with my figures so at this stage he called his deputy in to the room to and told him what had happened and had to reluctantly agree after a double-check that I was right.

After the meeting, I went back into my room that afternoon feeling quite pleased with myself that things had worked out in my favour, not wishing to contemplate what would have happened if he had found a mistake in my accounts. The next morning to my surprise the MD walked into my office and invited me out to coffee with him, well, I did not know what to think, his entire demeanour had changed and he was a very different person, I realised that I had obviously proved myself to him without knowing it.

It was only a few days later that I learned from some of the other staff that the MD would never interview an Asian or black person and they were extremely surprised at his new found friendship with me. It only goes to show that although prejudice may exist in people's minds it can be overcome by the real life experience and a breakthrough in communication

this can be brought about by ordinary events. I can honestly say that this was the only occasion that I felt discriminated against, but have never put it in the forefront of my thought process.

I must finish off this episode by saying that this particular MD would never have anyone else except me look after his accounts and audit, he subsequently offered me the job of being his chief accountant two years later, and was most disappointed that I could not accept.

My employment at Blick has continued to prosper as I became a manager and had my own team, directly responsible to one of the partners, but due to personal domestic reasons, I needed to increase my income, because of a pending move and the purchase of a new house. I decided that I needed to seek an increase of salary and saw my boss about it, I offered to take on more responsibility and all that goes with it, and although the meeting went well with excellent future prospects, I needed some action and a substantial increase in income now.

I went down to the audit room bitterly disappointed that I would have had to put my personal plans on hold, and in a fit of pique I asked all my colleagues if anyone knew of jobs going. It was customary for jobs in industry to be offered to qualified or senior accountants by clients because they could have direct recommendation of whom they were employing. I was very surprised when some shouted across the room that one of the clients, The Wesley Group, a large industrial firm, was looking for a chief accountant. I immediately went over and asked for the details. I got these and made the phone call without any delay and was invited to an interview in two days' time

I prepared for this somewhat unsure if I really wanted to move, but reminded myself the reason for initiating the change in the first place and proceeded to the interview, not realising that this was in itself going to be an experience of a lifetime.

When I walked into the interview room there were two people already sitting there, a large man and an elderly lady, who were introduced to me as the chairman of the company and the finance director of the company. The finance director did all the talking and the chairman simply sat there listening.

The interview began by the lady telling me about the company, the role they wanted of the chief accountant and their expectations in terms of improvements etc.; she also questioned my qualifications and experience, and whether I could deliver their needs, naturally, I confirmed that I had all the requisites for the role and elaborated on my abilities. Finally, it came to the salary requirements and I told them what I would be expecting as a starting salary in industry, which was approximately 50% more than I was getting in my present job in the profession. The lady sat back in her chair and started laughing out quite loud as if it were a big joke and then she told me what she thought the salary would be.

I was totally taken aback by this unexpected demonstration of what I thought was a cheek and also bad manners. My irritated response to her was simply to say that I had a perfectly good job where I was and was fully appreciated by my employer and therefore not interested in the offer. I stood up and prepared to leave the room. At this point the chairman stood up asked me to sit down again and took over the talking of the interview, he said that he would make me an offer which was to pay me almost what I was asking for immediately I joined and after my trial period of one month he would increase it to the higher figure which I had wanted. I thought about it for a few seconds and agreed, we shook hands, including the finance director, who had stayed silent during the conclusion of the deal – once again I made up my mind on the toss of a coin as it were and my life had changed direction, almost as if I was not full in control and it was almost dictated by life forces or fate, who knows?

The reality of the situation was that I had left the profession, landed a job in industry and become the chief accountant of a commercial company in my first job outside the profession, not bad going I thought, but now I had to deliver!

8.

Learning Business in Industry

I had to work my notice period at Blick's and when I saw Bob Glatter the next day to explain the position he was disappointed, but understood my situation and reasons for the somewhat sudden decision on my part, he was pleased that I was joining one of the firm's clients and wished me luck with the move.

My final month in their employ was both sad and filled with excitement at the prospect of my new position in industry as the chief accountant of a somewhat large company with interests in manufacturing, finance, shipping and a large property portfolio. I was extremely lucky to get the top finance job in an industrial company straight out of the accountancy profession, I knew this and was determined to make it a success, most of all because they needed a tough accountant to sort out the systems and I needed to prove myself as being completely in charge of the department, so it was no exaggeration to say that we needed each other at that time.

Starting in industry was going to be totally different environment to being in a professional office surrounded by other accountants and trainees who were either qualified or studying; one was never far away from a second opinion on any technical matter. In industry one becomes the ultimate point of reference on any technical matter and the degree of self-reliance comes to the fore, especially in the position as the chief accountant of the company, the financial buck stops there.

I need to describe my immediate boss, who shall be known as Miss Beata, the finance director of the company; she was a formidable character in her sixties and a spinster with loads of practical experience in industry and had in the past been with the occupation forces in Germany after the Second World War and did not suffer fools gladly, you will remember my first meeting with her at my interview. In addition she never minced her words and told things as they were to everybody. I learned many things from her that were practical and full of common sense, which helped me immensely throughout my later working life and I think contributed immensely to my entire approach towards clients and the way I ran my accountancy practice in later years.

This being the case, I was met by her at reception on my first day and taken to the accounts department. Shock horror, I was led into a large office with about ten desks and was shown to one of two very large desks in the centre of the room. I was somewhat shocked and disappointed that I was not led into my own private office with a nameplate marked 'Chief Accountant'. Also to my surprise I was sitting opposite Miss Beata, my immediate boss. Open plan offices had not arrived in the business world and generally, all important officers of companies had their own space or so I thought. At lunchtime that day, as soon as I was on my own with Miss Beata, I complained that I was expecting my own office as I was the chief accountant and needed the privacy. She slowly said all in good time Mr A, you need to sit among everyone for at least six months so that you know who works hard and who knows what they are doing, after that you can lock yourself in your ivory tower and be the 'Chief Accountant'. I hated every word she said, but came to realise how right she was not very long after.

Practical business management lesson No. 1:
"Listen and learn where it all happens"

I did not have to wait more than a few weeks after I joined the company to face my first test as the chief accountant which came in the form of a minor rebellion which I think was organised by the senior bookkeeper who had unsuccessfully applied for the job that I had, because he always seemed reluctant to carry out any instructions I gave him. The department comprised fourteen members of staff including me and the finance director, and he seemed to constantly egging others to argue with me. One afternoon I asked the sales ledger clerk to carry out a function which and she refused point blank to do for some unimportant reason and threatened to walk out, the whole department seemed to enjoy listening and watching the confrontation; the bookkeeper in particular. Faced with the threat to my authority and the threatened walkout, I told the sales ledger clerk to leave if she could not carry out my instruction she would have to carry out her threat, but if she did, I would not need her again and would not have her back; she collected her belongings and walked out.

I calmly walked over to her desk took the sales ledger from there over to my desk and told the rest of the office that if anyone else wanted to join her they could do so... The room was silent and no one budged. The next morning the sales ledger clerk came into the office and asked if she could have the ledger back and I responded that as she had walked out I had taken her function over and had no further need for her, so she left. A little while later Miss Beata walked in and asked if she could see me in private, I agreed and we went into a private room where she asked for the sequence of events that led to the dispute of the previous day as she had not been present.

I was told that the young lady was a very good worker and although a bit hot-headed was very reliable worker and that I should reconsider having her back. I explained that she had challenged my authority very publicly and that I was not prepared to let the incident pass without some action, and that it would be a lesson to all the others who thought that I would be a soft touch I was sticking to my guns. I discovered that the young lady was a favourite of Miss Beata, because she was a good worker, but I did admire the fact that although this may have been the case she did not try over-rule my decision, instead she suggested that the ledger clerk take the rest of the week off and I should think about it.

Although I never mentioned the incident outside the room, it had got to the hearing of the managing director and I was called into his office. As I entered he said Mr A I understand that you have had a little trouble in the accounts department to which I replied, yes a little problem, but nothing that I can't handle, he wanted me to know that I had his full backing and that I could get rid of all of them if I wanted to, something that was good to hear, even though the mere suggestion of such a situation could not arise with the current employment rules. Nevertheless, it was comforting to know that my bosses backed me fully and that I had their confidence after such a short time.

The following week, I had a meeting with the ledger clerk and amidst pleadings from Miss Beata, I agreed to take her back on the explicit understanding that it was her final chance and one more incident of insubordination and she was out for good. This was the only time during my six years with the company that any member of staff ever challenged my authority.

Practical business management lesson No. 2:
"Do not ever be afraid to stand your ground"

Although I had a good working relationship with my boss I always found her directness and abrupt manner somewhat irritating and hard to tolerate so whenever she annoyed me with what I considered to be rude I ended up by swiping and being sarcastic in my responses to her, and although it did not make for a very harmonious working relationship I learned how to deal with abrasive individuals.

I recall another incident when she asked me to organise the filing system in the general office, which was adjacent to the accounts office. I was both flattered and pleased to show off my knowledge of office organisational skills and proceeded to accomplish this task with all I had learned in my training. When I had completed the task, I went in to see her and asked her to check it out fully expecting her to tell me how wonderfully I had done the job. She took her time checking it out and finally came into my office to tell me what she thought; I waited in self-gratified expectation for her to thank me for the wonderful function I had performed.

Miss Beata stood in front of my desk with the thumbs of both hands in tucked into the waistcoat she was wearing and tutted for a moment, then she said very deliberately, "Mr A you have done a wonderful job and installed a very sophisticated filing system; the only thing is that you did one thing wrong." "What is that?" I inquired. She responded that the filing clerk was not a chartered accountant and was a school leaver from East London. I was furious; I could have got up from behind my desk and strangled her then and there with my bare hands… But the truth of the situation was that she was absolutely right and I had not considered the end user of the system.

Practical business management lesson No. 3:
"Make sure the end user is able to use the system"

Although I crossed wires with Miss Beata on most days, I had a sneaking respect for her very hands-on practical approach and the common sense solutions that she advocated and constantly came up with arising everyday situations in the company, and although I never fully appreciated the experience I was gaining at the time, I certainly owed her a lot, especially when I set up in business on my own later on.

We quarrelled often and disagreed all the time about manner and approach on many things, but we must have cultivated a healthy respect for each other's strengths and abilities, this was brought to light suddenly when one evening she asked me if I could give her a lift to the station on my way home from work. I agreed.

Nothing more was said until we got into my car and as soon as I closed the door she told me that she had something very important to discuss with me. What is it I enquired and she looked at me very tearfully and said Mr A I think I have got cancer in my stomach. I asked her reassuringly, why do you think that and have you seen a doctor? She replied not, but said that she had symptoms and knew that something was wrong and that she had a lump in her stomach. I told her that I had Harley Street connections and that I would find her a very good consultant who she could visit and get the situation clarified. I did this over the next few days as a matter of urgency and gave her the name and details of whom she should see.

Miss Beata saw the consultant and was admitted to St Bath's hospital for exploratory surgery. The day after the operation I visited her and was greeted by her as I walked in introducing me to the nursing staff with the words "This is the man who saved my life." It appeared that there was a non-malignant growth which had been removed and all was well, this one incident cemented our friendship and her entire attitude towards me changed; not only her manner but also the way we worked together.

I had worked in the company for just over two years and had accomplished the task of computerising the department and improving all the systems and had delivered most of what was expected. I had not had a meeting or review of my position with my Chairman, this although I had been given the higher of the two starting salaries as promised. I was getting a little restless and felt that there was nowhere obvious to go in the company, I discussed the scenario with one of the senior directors Mr Rainstorm who had adopted me as his prodigy for no obvious reason, and he told me that he thought there was no automatic prospects for any young ambitious man and that he thought it was a case of 'dead man's shoes' as regards promotion for me within the Wesley Group. Mr Rainstorm had some curious sayings and he left me with a thought that I still use today. "If you think you are indispensable to the company, think again! The world's cemeteries are full of indispensable people." Now that is a thought!

With this in mind I asked the chairman if I could see him for a chat to which he replied that he would come back to me with a date and time. Two weeks passed by and nothing happened, I therefore reminded him again and had the very same reply another two weeks passed by still no appointment and it got to the point that I reminded him about six times with no response. I was extremely unhappy at being put off with such a paltry excuse that I contacted a recruitment consultant with whom I had been acquainted and went along for a chat at his offices in Bond Street.

The conversation went well and he told me of an American company who were looking for a London-based European financial controller who would have to travel to Paris, Brussels and Milan once a month and run all four offices, and wanted to know if this position may have been of interest to me. The starting salary package was to be double what I was getting and a company car was to be one of the perks as well. I did not need to think too long or hard about it and decided that I would like to proceed with having an interview with the American chairman and the British director of the company.

The interview went extremely well and I learned that the company's head office was based in Buffalo, New York State and they were a leasing company. I was asked some technical questions on how I would account for write off of rolling stock etc. and must have answered correctly as the position was offered to me, I explained that I had a three months' notice period and unless I was asked to leave sooner they would have to wait three months. I was pleased to hear that they would wait for me. I accepted the job and went into the office and handed in my notice, in the hope that I would be asked to leave immediately.

My chairman was adamant that I would have to serve the full three months so that he could find a replacement and from that day one he stopped talking to me as he saw it as an act of disloyalty to him and the company. Time went on and I was making sure that all the people in my department were fully briefed to take over with little or no disruption, after I left. Miss Beata was most upset that I had handed in my notice and had been to see the chairman to tell him that he should make sure that I stayed

One Friday evening before my date of departure I was invited to have an after work drink at the local pub which we frequented, by some of the managers in the company and I accepted. The chairman turned up at the bar as he usually did and to my surprise he talked to me for the first time in many weeks. Some drinks later, one of the managers asked when I was leaving the company and the conversation led on to why I had decided to leave and that perhaps I should change my mind and stay with the company; the conversation group increased and was eventually joined by the chairman. They all turned on the pressure on me to change my mind and the chairman went on to tell me that he had promised his mother that he would open a private bank and that when he did this, I would be the obvious choice to head the operation. It was all very flattering to my ego and it did make me think that perhaps I should change my mind; however I had given the American company my word that I would join them and I felt obliged to stick with these arrangements. The reality of the situation was that the carrot dangled in front of me by everyone was casting doubts on what I really wanted.

That evening passed and I decided to consult my uncle, who was my guru at the time and we discussed all the options at length. His final bit of advice to me on the matter was that "The job of financial controller with the American company was something you could get if one was available at any time, whereas being the chief financial man to a tycoon was not a position you will come across very easily," and he thought it was something I should consider seriously, this I did over the weekend and when I arrived in the office on the Monday I made an appointment to see Mr Kurtman, my chairman, that afternoon I went into his office and told him exactly what my position was.

I first asked him if his offer for me to stay on as his number one financial man of the previous Friday was a serious one and if it was still on the table, once he confirmed this I told him that the American company had offered me double what my present salary was and a company car as well and that I would only consider changing my mind and staying at the Wesley group only if he matched the full financial package that I had been offered as the financial controller of the American company. He thought about it and reluctantly agreed. I then also told him that as far as I was concerned, he had to accept that it was the start of our new deal and that I did not want him to think that he could match their offer and then forget about me for the next five years. He was not happy, but agreed and I left his office thinking that had he met with me before I looked for another job it would have cost him a huge amount less.

Practical business management lesson No. 4:
"Don't wait until someone finds another job if you want to keep them, make sure they get recognition in pay and conditions"

Naturally, I was extremely pleased with myself as was Miss Beata because I was going to stay as the CFO of the company, but I still had the task of telling the American company of my change of mind and battled with an inner feeling of disloyalty because I felt that I had let them down. Needless to say, they were not very happy and neither was the recruitment consultant, who lost his placement fee. I consoled myself with the thought that they would have done the same if they had a better offer, I had to do what was right for me. Filled with the euphoria of my new prospects in the company and understanding of all the promises the chairman had made to me, I directed my immediate attention to choosing a company car within the given budget.

9.

A Second Phase in Industry

My new deal with The Wesley Group had begun and I was full of enthusiasm to become the right hand man of Mr Kurtman, who, in fairness, apart from being very wealthy was an extraordinary entrepreneur in his own right and had grown the company from a shell to what it was now. He was a sales oriented person and in some respects only respected wheeler dealers, who could turn a profit on a deal, administrators and accountants in his mind were simply a necessary overhead. I realised this very on in our relationship, which remained very formal throughout my working life with him.

Monthly management accounts, cash flow statements and such were treated with a degree of scepticism and although he took these form me he never commented on them very often, occasionally he would come into my office and tell me that something looked incorrect, in every such instance he was invariably right and therefore I had a great commercial respect for his ability to know exactly what was what in the financial sense, although he was not any kind of an accountant he just had a sixth sense about business and profitability.

Naturally, he expected me to deliver everything that I was paid for as his CFO and all he wanted from me on a daily basis was a summary of all the bank balances, the total debtors, the total creditors and the daily exchange rates for the major currencies. In addition to this he signed every cheque that was paid when he was in the country, otherwise when he was abroad any one of two directors and I had to sign all cheque payments. I observed that signing the cheques and my daily summary kept him totally abreast of the finances of the company at all times. On every occasion that he queried anything he turned out to be absolutely right. I have always advocated a similar set of financial controls to any business owner, so that they were aware of their general finances, whether they were finance orientated or not. Lesson in

Practical business management lesson No. 5:
"No one can be more interested in a business' finances than the owner"

Having realised that the only way to get closer to Mr Kurtman was through entrepreneurship I made sure that I shared any thoughts I had on the stock market, the currency market, the commodity market, the property market and of course the price of oil and gold. I would say that he appreciated this more than any of my other CFO duties, because from time to time he asked for my views on commercial situations. I honestly would not know what he thought of them because he was never a man who would share or discuss his thoughts and always made his own financial decisions.

Usually when I heard about anything new he was doing it was to tell me what he had done, rather than tell me he was thinking about doing it and asking for my view, I have to say that I found this very frustrating and left me feeling outside in the cold.

I began to realise gradually that I was unlikely to ever become the financial right-hand man that I was promised I was going to be and of course hoping to be, particularly because that was what I changed my mind about and stayed on at Wesley for. Having said that, I also need to say that I had to follow the course for some time and wait for some or any of his promises to become a reality.

After a further two years, I had established myself as a respected and senior member of the company and had brought about many changes and ideas for the benefit of both the management and the staff and hoped that in view of my contribution, I may have been invited to join the board and be offered the position of finance director, but there was no sign of anything to come. All the staff and other directors alike treated me as a source of ultimate reference and I became the de facto head of admin and personnel which I absolutely loved, but I still craved a higher challenge.

It was in this frame of mind that I approached Mr Kurtman one day and asked if I could meet with him to discuss our future together, he duly made the appointment and I went into his office where we sat down for an informal chat. I started to tell him that it was a further two years since he had asked me to stay with the company and I had not seen any dramatic changes to what had gone on before to which he replied, "Well you are the chief accountant, what more do you want?" I told him exactly what I had felt and that in reality I was a glorified bookkeeper apart from title and that the experience I was getting was the same as the first year and then repeated four times over, rather than moving on to bigger and better things. He asked me what I thought I wanted and I replied that I would like to think that I would be groomed to take over his role in time and be in a position to assist him to run the company. His answer was quite simple… "I am not going anywhere, so there is no need to groom anyone."

Our conversation ended in what was an unresolved manner and I left his office knowing that I really had no long term future in the company, sad but true! My work had become routine with no new challenges on the horizon, perhaps I had outgrown the company and the opportunities it could offer me. Mr Rainstorm was right; it was a dead man's shoes situation, no place for a young ambitious guy!

There was a basic structure of traders and directors all in their sixties in the company, and a group of younger executives and traders who were in their thirties and I had noticed the same a similar situation arising with some of the other young executives in the company as well. One particular bright younger trader had suddenly given in his notice and it was rumoured that he was setting up on his own in competition with the company. It was also rumoured that he had been asked to leave immediately and was banned from ever visiting the premises; in addition soon after this to everyone's surprise one of his other colleagues had also left to join him

I pondered my position at length and although there was no obvious and immediate answer, there were some developing opportunities on the horizon and although these did not appear to be any more than temporary advice situations some friends and acquaintances outside, who were in the business and commercial sectors and had asked me for some business and financial advice, which I gave them on a non-commercial basis. Without quite realising what this could lead to it had increased and due to my practical approach to business I was being approached to a greater degree than before.

During my stay at the Wesley Group I had also cultivated many banking connections with both merchant and the clearing banks in the normal course of business, and had a lot of exposure to arranging loans, buying and selling foreign currencies and seeking credit lines. During one such meeting I met a senior bank manager at the Allied Irish bank who was interested in financing the Wesley Group's activities through my connection with him and although the proposed deal did not come to fruition, without realising it at the time, I had made what was to be one of the most important banking connections in my commercial life.

Working life at the Wesley Group carried on as usual, although little minor irritations were creeping into the relationship between Mr Kurtman and me and while this situation continued from time to time, we had a somewhat serious incident that took place. One of the accounts department staff had made a mistake with a good customer of the company and Mr Kurtman told me that he was extremely unhappy about it, he came into my office and told me that the member of staff concerned was never to be given a pay review again and that he was considering giving her the sack. Of course as the CFO, I took full responsibility for the mistake and told him that I would institute a system to ensure that a similar error would not happen again; he left my office and went to lunch.

After lunch, he was walking past my office once again and this time he decided to stand outside the door and in a very raised voice take me, the member of staff concerned and the whole accounts department to task. The shouting at the very top of his voice, this went on for a several minutes and suddenly something inside me snapped, this was simply not on I thought. I walked to the door of my office and shouted back...

"How dare you stand in the corridor shouting at me... if you have something to say come into my office shut the door and tell me about it. If you do not treat me with respect, how do you expect my staff to, I know you own this company, but you don't own me... if you want to sack me you can but you cannot shout at me like this and don't you dare forget that!"

The entire corridor went silent, Miss Beata had come out of her room and was trying to calm me down, Mr Kurtman went silent and walked back to his office, this was a defining moment for both of us he never shouted at me again and my relationship with him changed for good. The fact was that he did not sack me and the incident was never referred to again I have never allowed anyone to treat me with indignity since then and I would never try to take anyone's dignity however mad I get.

The long-term consequence of that confrontation was that it was to be the foundation of my seeking pastures new, although I did not know it at the time. The Allied Irish bank manager I referred to earlier was a senior manager and had a large network of clients and colleagues who respected him, and it was through one of these connections that a retired Bank manager suggested that we should consider going into business together. He was to provide the business connections and potential clients and I was to undertake the accounting work and financial advice.

Although I was not entirely happy with the situation at the Wesley Group, it was a good, well-remunerated job and I had run things for almost six years in total, I had accepted that there were no immediate prospects and that I was not going to be heading Mr Kurtman's 'new ventures' that he had talked about. I had also toyed with the idea of going into business on my own, but not planned anything concrete or definite, especially since it meant giving up a secure salary and living on savings until the business started making profits.

It was around this time that one afternoon, Mr Kurtman came into my office and was going through some papers with me and when I replied to one of his questions he simply 'tutted', quite rudely I thought... after our meeting I asked him if he could spare a few minutes and he asked abruptly "what is it?" I replied with great delight that I wanted to leave the company and to give him three months' notice. He sat back in his chair and I watched the colour drain from his face, after collecting his thoughts he asked what I was going to do, I told him that I was going to set up my own business an accountancy practice. His response was that setting up in business was risky and advised me against it also reminding me that I had a good job with his company

Once again by almost the toss of a coin my life and career path had changed direction completely without any long period of planning. I had left the accountancy profession to go into Industry and now by almost a twist of fate or destiny I was going back into public practice as an accountant, this time in my own right. It would be a gamble, perhaps a little premature and unexpected, but it was going to be my own business decisions and I was going to call the shots. I recall that I was once told by an astrologer that I would be a successful businessman, was this the moment and was it likely to be true or was this going to be my wrong decision?

I gave in my formal notice in due course and my official time of leaving was to be at the beginning of February. My secretary at the time, Janice, who had helped me initially with all of the typing and completion of some of the clients' work at her home in the evenings and at weekends after work decided that she would also leave and offer her services to my new proposed business venture; I was more than a little reluctant to accept her offer because I had no obvious means to pay her an initial salary, but she insisted that she would be prepared to take the gamble with me and that if things did not work out she would then simply have to find another job, rather than miss the opportunity of being with me and the new business from the start. Janice proposed that as she lived with her parents at home her train fares and a small weekly allowance would suffice because if she did not make the move there may have been a missed opportunity for her too, and I may have found a replacement in the meantime who would have kept the permanent position. After much discussion I agreed to take Janice on and take a chance on how things would work out, fortunately for both of us things did get off to a flying start.

10.

Going it Alone

During my notice period at the Wesley Group, many people who had sought 'one off' advice from me earlier, either professionally or as a friend decided they would now become clients of my newly formed practice, which I named Ian Anthonisz & Co. chartered accountants

Call it what you like, but I feel that good fortune or fate played a great part in the very early success and the growth of the practice and the somewhat meteoric intake of clients during my first year in business. My chance meeting of one such client whose name was Barry Spencer. He was introduced to me by a professional contact Kym Edwardo, who was working for Barry as his accountant but wished to give this work up due to the pressures of his day job and offered to 'sell' him on to me which was common practice with accountants, and their client base did so on the understanding that I paid him a percentage of the fee on a monthly basis during the first two years of my services to Barry.

Being the personality that I was, I saw this as an excellent opportunity in terms of starting my own practice and had no objection whatsoever to paying what was, as I saw it, effectively an introductory fee, I grabbed the chance of having my first new big client and negotiated the basis of payment of the commission to Kym, my business contact, and immediately began working for Barry, as his accountant and Janice my assistant helped with the bookkeeping on a weekly basis. The relationship with Barry grew very strong in a comparatively short time together with social outings and what I can only term as mutual growth of both our businesses.

One evening during this time Barry and his partner confronted me at dinner and asked me quite directly if I had paid Kym a fee for the introduction and if I was still paying him a commission of any sort. I tried to avoid the question because I did not wish to lie about something which was true so I told Barry that it was customary for accountants to pay for practice goodwill. Barry was extremely annoyed, I would say even furious that I was paying Kym for the transfer and told me that if I continued, he would leave me as a client immediately. Not knowing how serious he was I contacted Kym the very next day, to my surprise Kym already knew that one of his friends had told Barry about our agreement, during a drinking session with Barry. Knowing my predicament Kym decided that he did not want any further payments from me and wanted me to keep Barry as a client, this meant that I bought Kym's practice for just a few months payments instead of twenty-four monthly payments, quite obviously a cash flow bonus for me beyond any reasonable belief and managing to please Barry without falling out with Kym either.

Little did I know at the time that Barry would have the largest bearing and impact on the early growth of the practice; he was an actor's agent by profession and very theatrical in personality, within a very short time he began to rely on me for all his business and financial advice and really appreciated what I did for him and his organisation. The result of this was that he introduced me to many of his contacts and other film and theatrical businesses including casting directors, actors and actresses, and other agents with whom he moved about socially some of whom became clients of my practice. One of the more special of these introductions was to his solicitor Andrew, who himself specialised in showbiz clients.

The introduction to Andrew was to be one of the best professional links I was to have for me and my practice. Andrew became my solicitor and we built up a long lasting relationship of trust and understanding of professionals with each other and were able to make mutual introductions to each other whenever one of our clients needed the services of a competent solicitor or a business advisor. Over the next fifteen years, we sent each other what seemed like an unending stream of clients, some of whom are still with the practice and with me.

Barry also offered me the use of the entire basement of a china shop he owned called 'Sam's Kitchen' as my first office on the basis of my being available to him at short notice as his own office was very close by, needless to say I gladly accepted his offer and we went about making the basement look as professional and upmarket as we could. Much to everyone's surprise it looked very professional and welcoming.

I always believed that my shop window had to convey the message that we were serious players in business and that we catered for the higher end of the market. I think that I owed this value to the fact that I did my training at Stoy

Hayward which always portrayed the image of being a posh and exclusive professional firm, whereas had I done my original training at a small local firm my entire view of the profession would have been somewhat different.

Meanwhile the retired bank manager who had originally suggested that we went into business together wanted a slightly different arrangement to what he originally planned, the new arrangement being that he kept his own clients and paid me for the accountancy and tax work that I did, we trashed out a workable arrangement to suit both of us, that way we both kept our own independence and clients and most importantly staff costs and overheads. The arrangement worked very well, until we had a somewhat major disagreement on the type of clients and type of work that we undertook, this ended the association and the arrangement we had, we parted company to our mutual satisfaction, but not entirely amicably.

My association with Barry was going to prove to be one of the most important business and social connections I was to make in my business life. Barry had an extremely outgoing personality and was a very colourful person. He also dominated most of his business and social connections and he enjoyed having me by his side during all business meetings and this gave me huge exposure to business contacts in day to day life that most accountants and business advisers would not have had. I would not be exaggerating at all to say that I met and knew most of the casting directors and actors' agents in London on first name terms at that time. I also had the good fortune to meet these people socially at dinners, parties, film premieres and such events, resulting in being able to talk to them on a one-to-one basis, resulting in some of them becoming clients of my practice. One of the funniest things he would do at any of his social get-to-gethers was to toast me as "A toast to my accountant and friend without whom, I would not be where I am today," this was quite flattering and perhaps a little embarrassing, but gave a very strong underlying recommendation to all present, which I am sure had a very positive effect on my practice growth.

During that first year of business, the practice comprised of Janice and me on our own, and we worked all hours to make sure that we serviced the clients well, giving them the best attention we could and ensuring that we were a one stop shop for anyone, we acted for. This created work for us and the early client relationships were most satisfactory from both points of view. As the business commenced in the middle of February the end of the first calendar year was only ten and a half months long and we had signed up fifty new clients, this was more than one a week and reason indeed to celebrate! Our target growth from then on was set as one client a week, making it fifty-two new clients a year. I have reflected on this achievement which we achieved plus or minus one or two clients during the first five successive years in business.

During this first year in business I realised that in order to attract the right type of growth, I needed to upgrade our premises into a larger and more prestigious looking office, which would give me a separate meeting or board room for formal meetings. After all my motto and target market was

"Aimed at the Discerning Client who Prefers Individual Attention"

and who were not catered for by the larger firms, and I had to compete with them on price and delivery. This is how we decided to become a niche firm offering a quality service.

The golden opportunity to acquire my own premises presented itself almost by accident, when Robert, one of Barry's colleagues mentioned to us that he had to sell his lease and release capital to acquire a flat for himself and his mother, but did not have the funds to buy his lease entitlement in the first place as he was a sitting tenant. It so happened that I had also thought his premises would have been perfect for me over a period of several months preceding this announcement by Robert. Once I heard of the situation I set about finding a tempting solution for him which would also give me the first refusal on his premises.

The solution I came up with was to lend him the funds to buy his lease entitlement and then immediately sell it to me at a fair market price which would give him a large profit, but also give me the property without having to go to the open market. Robert thought it was a perfect deal for all of us and the arrangement went ahead, resulting in him getting his capital and my getting my first own premises from which to operate. With all the humility of the world, I would like to say that I am at my best when "finding solutions for situations."

Apart from finding our next office, this deal was to be the beginning of my getting into the property market of the West End of London, not knowing at the time of course that property in the West End and central London was going to produce the greatest growth over the next twenty five years.

As a strategy, I have always believed that I would be better off in the long run buying a property rather than renting it, because from a cash flow point of view the loan repayments were almost the same as one would pay in rent and at the end of a given period I would own the property and also have the advantage of any possible capital growth. This philosophy has always paid off for me because over the years the capital growth, which even after paying the capital gains tax, has given me a percentage of growth better than any other use of funds. I have therefore always owned my office premises.

Having completed the deal we set about the refurbishment of the premises to make it have the look and feel we wanted to project to our clients, which was an upmarket firm which may have been small but believed in delivering a quality service of individual personal attention, a strategy that I think we have certainly achieved over the years.

Looking back to this period of the growth of the firm, I like to recall some of the outstanding introductions and the good fortune we had signing up some very notable clients, most of which came from semi-social contacts. Barry had introduced me among others to a Harley Street consultant doctor who had a huge practice and following some months of social meetings ended up becoming a client of mine for many years and still remains so, this connection opened doors to an entire new world on both the professional and social scene.

I also met up with a very local firm of solicitors, with whom I developed a close professional relationship and we were able to make many mutual introductions, resulting in some very big client referrals for the practice. Among these was a Danish financier who had lots of connections with the Middle East and as he was very satisfied with the work that I did for him, he in turn recommended me to some big Kuwaiti and Saudi clients, who had started big businesses in central London.

Among the new introductions to the practice was a Saudi princess who owned a well-known private hospital in London. Once again it happened through a chance meeting with an old friend of mine whose name was Roland Appuhamy, whom I met on the street in Marylebone and he was being accompanied by his boss, the managing director of the hospital owned by the princess, after we had met me a few times and began to rely on me for advice on all matters financial and strategic planning for the hospital and soon he wanted me in on all his important meetings.

The hospital had some very well-known consultants working there and he wanted to project the right image to both the British medical establishment and of course the Middle East from where they marketed the hospital for their patients. Because he thought I was a social asset to the promotion of the hospital, I was invited to some of the most prestigious venues in the capital one such outstanding place at the time was Les Ambassadeurs Club, which I had only heard of from the James Bond films and was privileged to accompany my client as his co-host on many occasions. I can honestly say that in the normal course of work I would not have had access to this level of social platform as it was the domain and reserves of only the very wealthy or famous.

The princess who owned the hospital also relied on my participation on matters financial and strategic relating to the running of the hospital and I developed a good and close working relationship with her. In all these matters I learned that trust was the most important part of a business relationship and I do believe that my clients trusted both my advice and opinions. Whenever the princess was in London, I was invited at least once to dinner at her residence, where I was treated very much as a VIP with other selected guests.

I think that I need to mention that social exposure at all these levels matured me as an advisor to clients at all levels of the spectrum, because I while I was lucky enough to meet the rich and famous, I also had small shop keepers in East London with whom I would visit to sort out their VAT and have a cup of tea with, and at the same time as I would be wined and dined at some of the most desirable venues in the capital. I always considered it a privilege to work for everyone and I am proud to say that I visited everyone personally and was able to give them advice to suit their situation and needs at whatever level was necessary.

Around this time, I was introduced to an interesting client Saleh Al-Doni who was of either Jordanian or Iraqi origin; he was a professional "fixer" who had lived in London for some time and was able to source all necessary introductions to his wealthy Middle Eastern clients. He would source the services of Harley Street doctors and consultants, specialist lawyers, property agents and of course accountants to visiting rich Middle Eastern people. This client again changed the outlook of the practice. Because of his connections, he was able to introduce me to many Middle Eastern businessmen who travelled to the UK and had their businesses in London. Most of them needed a business advisor who they could rely on; I was pleased to fill the gap and expand the growth of the practice.

Al-Doni was a perpetual visitor to all the London casinos and was well known to all of them because, apart from being a patron, he was one of the most successful introducers of Middle Eastern clients to the casinos, and was held in very high regard by all of them. The downside of the connection was that I had to have dinner with him several times a week. At first I felt lucky and was pleased to have the privilege of being taken out to dinner at some of the most prestigious places in London, but, not being a gambler of any sort, I simply had to dine out a lot instead. In addition to this, I was made a VIP member of most of the top casinos simply because I was his accountant and where I was invited to have complimentary lunch or dinner or both at any time. Needless to say I never took up the invitation, unless I accompanied the client simply because I did not gamble.

My connection with Saleh gave me the most incredible exposure to a lifestyle in London, enjoyed only by the extremely rich and privileged and I need to recall some of these experiences, because I know that many accountants and businessmen like me would never have had the opportunity to go out with to or meet the people I met and dined with in the normal course of business life, I can honestly say I was extremely lucky to have been in this position.

I would like to recall some of the more spectacular events that I experienced to share the fun and excitement that was available at the time. I was invited to the Ascot races and had a pass to the members' stand, at first I simply thought that it would be a fun day at the races where I would have a little flutter and come home in the evening. Al-Doni was to pick me up at eight o'clock in the morning, when I heard the car arrive I was more that surprised to see that it was a chauffeur-driven Rolls Royce and even more surprised when I got in to see that we were to have Dom Pérignon Champagne all the way there. Of course it was special but I did have a chuckle about how precious it was and that I could laugh about it.

When we got to Ascot we dined on an amazing luxury breakfast and prepared ourselves for the first stint of the races. The interlude was a few races and then we sat down to an absolutely scrumptious lunch followed by afternoon tea. On the way home it was DP champagne all the way once again and when I thought the party was over, the Rolls Royce stopped at the casino where I was a guest for a gourmet dinner, surely this was a day to remember. It is almost a shame that this level of entertainment and hospitality no longer exists in the business world.

One other event that I would like to recall was the Miss World final which was held in the Hilton Hotel on Park Lane where I was a VIP guest. The invitation included watching the completion followed a dinner where we had tickets to dine with the contestants and their chaperones; once again it was a night to remember and something for which I would not have been able to buy a ticket, all provided by my client connections, to say that I was fortunate enough to enjoy a privileged time was surely an understatement.

The practice and my client base had begun to grow at an amazing pace and it seemed that I was getting recommendations from existing clients, business associates and friends alike, and it was also noteworthy that the spectrum of the clients was very wide; this ranged from small businesses on the lower side to high net-worth individuals and some larger corporations, something which I had not fully expected and was very pleasantly surprised with. I have always had an inclination to help people who are underprivileged or bullied by the authorities or the system, therefore although I had an amazing social lifestyle by courtesy of my very wealthy clients I always had time for everyone else, especially the ones who found difficulty in paying the normal fee rates, so I discounted them whenever I could and they stuck with me for many years some over twenty years as clients.

One of the things I have reflected on is that when during the time I was a sole practitioner and personal business advisor as opposed to the head of a firm of accountants, my involvement with all my clients was so much more on a one-to-one basis that most of them wanted me to be present in person at every important meeting or function of theirs and while this was difficult in terms of a time commitment, I was extremely lucky that Janice was totally capable of keeping the office work up to date and certainly did.

I also kept myself professionally up to date and whenever necessary brought in expert advice for specific problems that may have arisen with special situations; whenever I engaged a specialist on behalf of a client I made sure that I accompanied my client to the consultation or meeting and understood the advice and opinion of the expert; this had an added advantage of giving me one-to-one exposure with competent specialists, thereby increasing my own knowledge and experience. It was also something that helped me to develop as an all-round professional advisor.

At the end of my second year in business our workload was so high that we used to work extraordinary hours, with a day and night session to make sure that the delivery of work was on time. We named these sessions as 'Ghosters' because we would work all day from nine am to five-thirty as usual, then have a break for about two and a half hours to have some dinner, which would usually be a Wimpy and chips, and start work again at about eight-thirty and work through the night. I would then have some shut-eye so that I could see my first client at nine, the next morning.

Sometimes when I'm told I was very lucky with the business, I smile to myself and say well yes I have had a lot of luck but the ratio of luck to hard work was probably 85% to 15%. Having said that I have no complaints whatsoever about working as hard because it was always my aim to build the business. Of course I have been extremely luck with the 'Business Angels' that I have met in my life such as Kenneth Hume my original benefactor who got me into Stoy Hayward and Barry Spencer my first large client who worked so hard to promote me into the entertainment industry and into a very different social sector of British society, that would have been normally difficult to penetrate.

My family always considered me to be a bit of a dreamer because I always had high ambitions and always had a dream about where I wanted to get to and where I wanted to be in many aspects of my life. Furthermore, coming from a background of family who were always employees there was an ethos of job security and the idea that one should be satisfied with having a steady secure job and not necessarily to be the boss.

I do clearly remember that even when I was relatively young I always wanted to be the 'Boss' whatever that was, and to be able to make the ultimate decision as to the direction in which I wanted to steer the company or business in which I was involved. I never had the inhibitions that seemed to restrict both my own father and my stepfather when it came to their lot in life. I also remember that on one occasion in a family discussion or argument my stepfather saying, "Son you know your problem, most people aim for the moon, but in your case you seem to want to aim for the stars. I really don't know what your problem is." I never quite understood what he meant, except that I thought that he was limited by his own expectations of life and that he felt success was being content with your position in life.

Another time a good family friend remarked that I would always be disgruntled because she thought that I always wanted something more or better. Again I never understood what she meant and remember feeling really upset inside me that a family friend who was a teacher thought that of me, because she thought that I would always be dissatisfied with whatever I had.

However, as I got older I realised that this was really my driving force and that ambition had to be driven, and it was the hunger to succeed that drove me for whatever reason. This quality helped me as a young boy and later on after my road traffic accident, when I needed all my resources to come to the fore and of course later on in my career and business ambitions.

In fact I can date this characteristic right back to my childhood and the time when I owned my first bicycle, then my first car, I have always had a quest for something better. I can go back to a time when I was growing up in Colombo, I was about eight years old and while I was crossing the Galle Road which was the main road going through the city, I suddenly saw a beautiful red sports car which looked absolutely amazing and beautiful. Having enquired everywhere about the make and model I was told that it was a Mercedes 190 sports, and I immediately fell in love with it. I instantly made up my mind that when I grew up I was going to own a Red Mercedes sports car. As I mentioned before, my parents always considered me to be somewhat of a dreamer and that I had ambitions well above my station in life. But the good news was that I achieved that particular ambition quite soon after I started in business. The interesting thing to me was that all the cars I owned before that one, were only stepping stones until I was able to afford my dream car, my own Red Mercedes sports. Once I finally did I own it no other car mattered to me and I treasured it and used it for well over seventeen years, and realised that after I had achieved the goal of my dream car the model or make of my car was no longer a primary goal of mine.

Having a successful business had become my next goal and I threw all my energy into this venture, it was not just about making money, in fact it was a lot more complicated than that because I wanted to be recognised as a good trusted advisor and also an enlightened boss who was able to run a business properly, focussed on effective customer delivery.

Quite by accident around this time I was given the opportunity to visit Disneyland in California and I have to say that I was totally overwhelmed by it all not because it was a theme park but because I saw it as a perfect business model. The precision of the way it was run the culture of care and cleanliness and the way in which the organisation looked after things gave me an insight into how a business should be run and most importantly the degree of training the staff seemed to have really impressed me. What was more was that I noticed a degree of customer care that I had not seen in England and how paramount it seemed to be in this organisation. What was more was that this was implemented together with the necessary firmness to keep it held together properly.

I came back to the UK determined to run my business as close to the way in which Disneyland was run although on a minute scale of course, but it gave me a whole new and different outlook. In fact I told many of my clients for years that visiting the theme park was not just fun but that it was a business sabbatical and recommended it to everyone as something they had to do, if they were in business.

I also borrowed one of Walt Disney's famous sayings which is

"If you can dream it... You can do it"

I cultivated this saying as my business inspiration for myself and I believe that I have lived by the saying, throughout the years of running my various businesses; it also meant that there was always a way to realising ones dreams, in my opinion it always helps to have an encouraging motto to help with reinforcing ones drive force. I remember having a meeting with the famous lawyer Victor Mischon who later became Lord Mischon with a mutual client and as soon as I sat down it his office I was quite impressed to see a caption on the wall behind his desk which said *'It Can be Done'*; he was obviously a person who had a motto as well.

11.

My Vision of the Business

A vision for a business or any project can be defined as what one eventually wants to achieve. Political leaders will set out their vision for a country and businessmen or entrepreneurs will know where they want to get to. In short, without a clear vision one simply drifts on and has no standard by which to judge their performance, I always ask any of my business mentoring clients the question "Where do you want get to and what would you like to achieve?" Sometimes they tell me that they had never thought about that, which is surprising.

As far back as I can remember in my childhood or young adulthood, I have always had a clear idea of how I would approach a situation and whether it was a very simple task or something more complicated my target was to make things look good and be operated efficiently. In my younger days this may have simply been about toys or vision of how I would make something. Going back to my childhood in Ceylon when I was given a toy I kept it in immaculate condition and even years after use it always looked brand new, this was because I cleaned it and polished it and kept it in its original box, nothing unusual for many children but in comparison I was far more fastidious than my brother

David and it was something the whole family talked about, not in a complimentary way I must say – they all thought that I was mean and would not share my toys, the truth was that I did not want anyone to damage my things. This is still true right up today, things had to be looked after and look good. I do not allow anyone in the office to use my personal pens and have a pot of 'public pens' for use by any member of staff or visitors and has caused much amusement in the office and at home. The same principles applied to my personal office, desk and even my cars. One of my cars is over twelve years old but looks like it was driven out of a showroom recently and apart from the model changes one would never know how old it was. Although this is all absolutely I say it with my tongue in cheek and can smile at myself and my silly idiosyncrasies.

The same degree of interest and care went into anything I got involved with. During my early teens when we made our own toy revolvers or guns with rubber bands and pieces of wood stuck together, mine had to look the most realistic because I would not be satisfied until I improved it to the best of my ability, and looking back I realise that this trait has followed me throughout my life in most things I did, whether they were school projects, recreational projects or in later life during employment and then in running my business. I always had a vision of where I had to get to; it is not surprising that the family friend said that I would be disgruntled an always want something better.

It took me many years and well into my adult life that to recognise my traits and turn them into strengths rather than allow them to become weaknesses. I do genuinely think that one's strengths when overplayed become one's weaknesses; I could give many examples of this particularly in the lives of some of our world politicians and leaders. Strong leaders of many countries have ended up as dictators or been thrown out of office by going that one step too far. In order to avoid any controversy, I will leave it to you my readers to apply this test to the various captains of industry and our politicians and world leaders to prove what I am talking about. Equally those who recognise their strengths and weaknesses and apply them in a balanced manner will reap the greatest benefit.

Turning back to my own business, I had a hunger and a vision of where I wanted to get to and although I had a very small business in its infancy, I always knew that I had to aim to provide the best service at the most reasonable price; not the cheapest; not the most expensive, but the best value for money. I feel that I can honestly say that this has always been my aim and to a large extent been achieved, over the years. In addition we have always provided a much person-alised service to our entire client base, sometimes taken too far by the odd client. I need to illustrate this point with a story of a client who came into the office for an early morn-ing meeting and as he had been having a particularly dif-ficult time, I asked if I could get him a light breakfast to which he instantly replied "That would be wonderful... I would like to have some boiled eggs and toast soldiers." I stood there in the boardroom somewhat stunned in dis-belief at the request, but Janice having heard his request immediately said that he could and sure enough served him the boiled eggs and soldiers something that we or the client would never forget. Thank goodness this degree of person-alisation was not common place.

Having been trained in what was considered to be a 'Big Firm' I knew about the expectations of the quality of service to clients and the level of record keeping that was to be a minimum. I also had a lot of experience of how the various departments such as Audit, Taxation, Insolvency and Administration, were run and although I was only beginning as a sole trader at the time, I used this experience to organise myself on these well-established lines, since then I had served in a more senior role at Blick Rothenberg and in industry at the Wesley Group. All in all I did have a fair level of experience and in many fields; the rest was up to me.

I have to say that I had a very clear vision of where I wanted to get to, which was as a firm who catered for the smaller Businesses and who wanted individual attention, but were unable to get this from the larger firms and, where small local firms were not equipped or interested in doing it, to this end I set up my goals and my stall.

I was in Sri Lanka recently and passed by a flower shop which so looked stunningly attractive to the point that I went in and introduced myself to the manager because I wanted to compliment him on how stunning his shop looked. The shop was called 'The Orchidist' and they only sold orchid flowers and plants, the displays and colours were simply magnificent and one instantly knew that the owner and manager had a vision of where they wanted to be. I became a customer of the shop and got to know the manager and what made him tick, since then I have got to know them well and have confirmed that there was a very clear vision behind the success of their business.

I could go on about the many clients who I have dealt with over the years who have succeeded in their businesses because of their great breadth of vision and succeeded in building up very successful businesses in a relatively short time, unlike the others, many others, who have failed simply because they did not have a vision of what they wanted to achieve. Let it suffice for me to say that a clear vision becomes the driving force of a successful entrepreneur the task in hand. In my opinion too many people are embarrassed to think or talk about their vision, for fear of being judged or criticised by their peers.

12.

Doing Things My Way in Business

As I have mentioned earlier I had a clear vision of what the business was to be like; namely a niche business with large firm attributes and concepts, I thought therefore that if I wanted the outside world to consider me as such, I needed to make sure I was taken seriously and within a relatively short time I took steps to have a company logo and a proper brochure, which although very common now was relatively rare in small businesses; in fact I knew much larger concerns that had neither.

I was clear in my mind that this was all part of my 'shop window' and made sure that we had both. I am sure that many of my peers thought that it was somewhat arrogant and self-centred but I always thought that it was more a question of 'self-belief' rather than any kind of arrogance. I have imparted this to many clients whom I have mentored by telling them that if "they did not value themselves, then how could others too?" Many people confuse this with arrogance; this is clearly not the case – on the contrary I have always found that bankers and other institutions I have worked with viewed it as a sign of self-reliance and confidence in my approach to a project. Throughout the growth of the business I am glad to say that I never had any problems in borrowing funds for growth or any new projects, which I attribute to the fact that I had a clear plan of what I had in mind and was able to demonstrate to my bankers why the idea and the business concept was sound.

Strangely enough it was only at the commencement stage of the business that there was reluctance on the part of my bank manager to help me get started and this was with a bank that I had banked with since I began my training some fifteen years earlier. I was so annoyed that I immediately sought my other banking connections and to my surprise one of the connections that I had developed while at the Wesley Group came up with the goods. Not only were they willing to give me the funding but I got it on an unsecured overdraft on my personal guarantee. This was an amazing offer and I stayed with that bank for almost twenty-five years, most of it with the same bank manager.

My relationship with this bank manager blossomed over the years and we were to develop a relationship that was went from strength to strength in both directions inasmuch that I recommended a huge amount of good business to him and the bank and they were able to assist with both the working capital and the finance for me to buy every one of my business premises. I became quite well known at the bank and with the other managers through the banks social functions; I can say with some humility I was regarded both as a good customer and a prolific introducer of clients to the bank.

However, the saying that people bank with people was so true for me because my connection was suddenly broken when my bank manager had an internal move within the bank and was no longer in the branch system. I was suddenly thrown into what I thought was a wilderness and for one reason or another never felt treated in the same way.

The end of my relationship with this bank after so many years of mutually beneficial; trading and transactions eventually broke down when one of the new managers who had been assigned to look after me wanted some really unreasonable conditions incorporated into my facilities. My trading history and relationship had lasted over just short of twenty-five years and they were treating me as though I was a completely new account holder and a stranger to the bank. I found this completely unjustified especially in view of the number of times that I had more than come up with the goods on my own projects not to mention the numerous client introductions I had made giving the bank millions of pounds of business in both investment and lending. I decided that it was time to leave and seek banking elsewhere.

I was glad that during all these years I had cultivated and kept with other banking connections either through professional contacts or those of my clients. The connection that came about was one of the big five clearing banks and to my surprise the manager who was introduced to me was a woman who was a go-getter with a real eye for business and ambitious to get on herself. I thought that this was a stroke of luck and proved to be a great move. Once again it took me on a totally new path of banking and monetary success. Within a few weeks she had arranged all the facilities I had with my previous bankers and more and even improved the mortgage facilities I had on my property portfolio, strange how in life one door closes and another opens. My relationship with this manager went from strength to strength and along the way she opened many doors for me both in business and in my personal banking and financing needs. The lesson to be learned in business is that one needs to cultivate connections all the time whether needed or not at a given moment because institutions themselves change their rules and criteria both internally due to changes within an organisation and sometimes due to external circumstances, such as changes in national policy or at times of a credit squeeze. I learned this lesson well and was glad of it because history repeated itself many years later, that time I was more prepared for it and more confident of the outcome.

13.

Tragic Personal Setback

Although I had been overjoyed at the idea of starting my own business many members of my own immediate family had misgiving and reservations about the entire concept. I think this was because everyone in the immediate and extended family came from an employee background and I may have well been the first person in a few generations who actually set out in a business of my own. The security of being employed seemed to be the value of the day and as all the members of my family sought to have a 'secure job with prospects' as it was called, and when I announced that I was going into business on my own I had plenty of family advice that I should think again and why would I leave a sound position as chief accountant of an established company to take a chance of starting a new business on my own, given the uncertainties of market conditions and competing in the field?

I even had advice from the elders in Ceylon such as my grand uncle who was a lawyer there and who thought that there was a degree of disloyalty to my employers leaving a company that had been good to me to start up on my own. My father too who had been employed as a civil servant in Ceylon for most of his working life thought that the degree of risk should have to be very seriously considered. Of course I had considered the risks and the uncertainty but I knew that working where I was accepting the fact of the 'dead man's shoes' scenario, because my managing director and the entire board of directors were going nowhere else and my chances of promotion depended on when they retired or how long they lived, otherwise there was no vacancy. This scenario was pointed out to me by one of the directors who had taken a liking to me and had adopted me as some sort of a prodigy. He had many conversations with me telling me what prospects I had as an ambitious young man working in a company where all the higher officers were in later middle age and hanging onto their jobs. One of his other gems of advice to me was to remember what happened to indispensable people, a sobering thought Remember Ian, however important you think you are to any organisation, the worlds cemeteries are full of indispensable people," a saying that I have always thought about and remembered especially if I ever thought that I was too important to anyone.

All that being said, I decided that I was going to make it on my own and saw that it was the only way to determine my own success or failure and how I was going to control my own financial growth and ambition. I had made a better start than expected and for one reason or another, the growth of the business was conveyed to my father in Australia, where he had lived for about ten years and was just approaching retirement at the age of sixty-five. My father had previously visited me in England about eighteen months after my road traffic accident and now that he was contemplating his own retirement the thought of making a trip to England came up for discussion and my brother David and I decided that we would buy my dad and his wife their tickets to visit us in the United Kingdom. For me this was especially exciting because I could show him my office and update him with the growth of the practice, after all this was not something achieved by any member of the wider family and was something to crow about. Apart from that I had not seen Dad for more that fourteen years.

The plans were made and the waiting for the event had almost arrived my father and his second wife, were due to arrive in the UK on the Monday morning, I therefore decided to give my office a final clean and polish while making the comment with a chuckle that my Dad would be the first to help himself to my executive drinks' cabinet. The phone suddenly rang out of the blue and when I answered it was my brother David, he was struggling to speak and stuttered for a moment or two and finally said, *"Ian, I have some really bad news, Dad has just died of a heart attack."* He was on the way to the airport in Melbourne when he had some chest pains and was taken to the emergency department of Dandenong Hospital where he died while being examined and was telling the doctors that he was on his way to seeing his sons after fourteen years. The cause of death was left ventricular failure which had happened while he was in mid-sentence.

The news was totally shattering! Here was I preparing for his arrival at Heathrow and now a few moments later being told that I would never see or talk to him again. It was an unbelievable moment of my life. Why now? Could he not have lived a few more days or weeks months? I had so desperately wanted to meet him again, show him my office and let him know what I thought I had achieved, what was it all about? I still don't have an answer. I can only console myself with the thought that his anticipation and excitement might have been greater than the actual reality, no one will ever know!

14.

First Major Setback – Employing a Friend

It was several years since the practice started and the office was getting extremely busy, and although we were servicing all the clients satisfactorily I clearly needed some serious top end help if I wanted to expand the practice and enable it to have some serious growth, my eldest son had always wanted to follow in my footsteps and become a chartered accountant, and this was an ambition that had not wavered in any sense, since he was about eight years old, but he was several years away from being able to get qualified and adequate professional experience outside my practice for this to become any kind of a reality in my practice. A few years was also too long to wait.

The search for someone suitable proved to be extremely difficult. What I was finding was that the quality was simply not good enough, because most of the bright young people did not want to join a smaller company because of long-term job security and small firms could not compete with the 'big boys' either in terms of salary and perks or other fringe benefits.

The people who were available were really second class in terms of drive and ambition and I needed someone who was switched on and hungry. I have always been extremely fussy about the quality of service that we offered and delivered and having someone without that quality was simply not what I wanted. At this time, I had employed nine full-time and part-time staff all of them dedicated women, especially the ones with children and family commitments, they had amazing attitude and output. I had noticed that for some reason the women who worked with me seemed to juggle their lives and make a part-time role as good as people who were employed full time, I had and have eternal gratitude for their efforts in my company.

Just about at this time in the history of the firm I took a phone call from a guy I had trained with at Stoy Hayward, almost fifteen years earlier and to my amazement he was looking for a job, I suggested that we met up to discuss the matter and see what we had in common.

The meeting went well and it felt like the time in between our training days had hardly passed, we were buddies together talking about the old days and the clients we worked for, including our immediate bosses and their good, bad, weak and strong points. In fact it seemed like we were destined to meet up for the sake of my company. My friend told me that he had worked for a PR company and that he had been there for around ten years and that the only reason he was leaving was because he had just been divorced and he needed to make a new start and was keen to leave industry get back into the profession, all this seemed like music to my ears.

Almost immediately, I offered him the job as a manager second only to me as regards seniority and the chance of a partnership in the company. Furthermore, as I had known him for so long and not only trained with him we had been out socially for years I did not see any need to go through the receive formality of references and all the other enquiries that I would have normally made for any other new employees. I needed this heavyweight assistance and frankly could not wait for him to join me.

He informed me that he had spoken to his employer and although he had to give them three months' notice he would be able to join me in about three weeks' time, I was overjoyed to say the least and we met to discuss the finer details of the working arrangements.

The broad arrangements were that he would receive an amount of monthly drawings to meet with his living expenses and would receive 50% of the profit at the year-end to be paid to him as soon as all the outstanding fees had been collected. All parties were satisfied with the arrangements and he then asked if I could rise to providing him with a modest car on the company to replace the company car that he was going to lose. I had always provided my own car partly because I was a car enthusiast and partly because I did not want the business to have to support my hobby of somewhat special cars. Nevertheless he stressed that his requirement was to be only a modest car and I agreed.

All the formalities now having been solved, the date for his joining was agreed and we both looked forward to starting what we thought was going to be a profitable partnership.

The next few months went well and I was gradually handing over some of my day to day client work to my friend who was eager to please me and lighten my workload. I assisted him by telling him of the entire needs of particular clients and how I dealt with their work. The new arrangements seemed to work extremely well although most of the staff were not keen to be supervised by him. I put this down to the fact that they had all been used to one boss who was me, and there would have been a natural resentment for someone from outside stepping in and taking over, so as to say.

I encouraged both the staff and my friend each on their own to make the transition as smooth as possible and explained that the change was in the interests of the company and their own long-term prosperity. I am pleased to say that everyone gave him the chance and the immediate prospects for the business seemed good. I had already opened a branch office in North London and we were able to share the attendance between the two offices to supervise the staff and visit the clients. The clients obviously had the choice of having meetings in North London or in the central London offices it all added up to the growth and stature of the business.

The North London office had come about because we had needed more staff and space and it was impossible to house everyone in the existing office in town and many members of staff came from North London, therefore the location seemed obvious to me, apart from which I always preferred to buy premises rather than rent them.

My business philosophy was that owning a property usually cost the same as renting the space, but in my thinking owning the property strengthened the balance sheet and increased by property portfolio. There were in fact two separate businesses running side-by-side that of the accountancy practice and a property business for no extra cost. This philosophy has proved to be correct for me anyway to this day. I always referred to my property holding as my 'Pension Scheme'.

Having an extra pair of hands at the top end of the business certainly generated more growth for me as I was able to network more easily and between my friend and I we were able to rationalise many things I had not done before through a lack of time.

We took on a permitted financial services division and were able to grow this side of the business which produced additional revenue and seemed to excite my friend. I suppose the commission income was relatively easy to work because once an introduction was made the insurance company did all the chasing up until the policy was signed, and we reaped the share of the commission, something that does not happen now due to new regulation which came in subsequently. Nevertheless, It seemed that the investment in the new prospective partner was beginning to pay off.

At this time there were a few structural problems beginning to develop, which I had not realised was happening for one reason or another. My friend and I had formal monthly partnership meetings at which we discussed such issues as business revenue, client satisfaction, and work deadlines and of course internal partnership matters. One such thing was that my friend had not approved or in fact disputed my draft of the formal partnership between himself and me, although it was always on the agenda. Whenever I brought the matter up his response was that he was having domestic issues which took up his personal time and that he never had time to go through the draft properly. He always apologised and I would give him more time, this went on for several months now and although it did concern me I accepted his excuses put the matter on hold until our next partnership meeting. How silly and wrong I was!

Suddenly one morning, my friend announced that his divorce had come through and that he was getting married again and in view of the family situation it was going to be very low-key, simply the couple, two witnesses and immediate family.

I accepted this scenario at perfectly plausible and wished him all the very best. As the date approached he requested two weeks' leave for his wedding and a honeymoon that followed, of course I was totally agreeable and the event occurred, neither I or any of the office staff were invited, something we all accepted without question.

My friend had been with the company for fourteen months by now and in terms of work, things seemed to be going well, and then came the shock. While he was away I had a telephone call from one of the insurance company managers who was chatting to me generally about all things great and small when he said, "Ian I was a little surprised that you did not come to your business partners wedding, it must have been a little hard for him even though you were busy." This was an absolute shock to me in view of what I was told by him directly. I stayed silent for a moment and the pretending that I knew about it all the time found out everything that I needed to know about the situation and what I thought was a deception.

I thought all about the matter throughout that evening and could not figure out why my friend would invite some of our clients and business associates to his wedding and reception afterwards and not invite me or some of the staff at least. I understood that it was entirely his prerogative, but why lie about it to me? The more I thought about the more confused and angry I got about it, there must have been a bigger or different motive... There had to be because it simply made no sense!

After much soul searching and other enquiries from staff and clients I decided that I had no option to confront him with the matter immediately on his return to the office, without giving him any time to ponder about the matter or prepare any answers in advance. I therefore decided on a plan of action, no phone or other contact before he returned to the office, I also locked the staff entrance to the office and made sure that he had to come through the front door, where the clients normally entered the building.

The day of his return arrived and I had told all the staff that I would open the door to him; shortly before 9 am the door knocker went, I opened the door and as I said hello I invited him into the boardroom, telling him that I wanted to have a short meeting before he went downstairs to his office, he had no reason to suspect that I had an ulterior motive. I motioned him into the opened door of the boardroom and offered him a chair, asked him if he had enjoyed his honeymoon etc. I then casually told him that there was a slightly mysterious matter which I wanted to clear up before we talked about any work assignments. He agreed.

I mentioned that I had talked to Roy our business associate who told me that he was at the wedding and who was quite surprised that I was not there; I had to control my emotions as I felt a surge of anger pass through my entire body because of his obvious discomfort and uneasiness at hearing what I had to say. I controlled myself but spoke with some difficulty when I asked him for an explanation for his behaviour, especially because I had offered him a fifty percent share of the business and told him that this was not behaviour I would expect or want from a prospective partner.

The reply he gave me was even more shattering and totally unacceptable. He told me that he had got married to a woman only to get half a share of her house and that he had even taken his wedding ring off before he came into the office and that it was a marriage of convenience for him. It still did not answer why he had kept the whole thing secret from me and why while the clients and business associates were at the wedding and why he told them I was too busy to attend. Everything was a complete lie.

I felt that everything about his behaviour was unacceptable and not a basis for our continued partnership and I told him so in no uncertain terms; I also told him that I was going to suspend him pending further enquiries and consideration by myself. I then opened the boardroom door and told him to leave immediately, at this moment I had not realised what else I was going to find out within the next few hours and how the episode was going to end.

Soon after he left the building I phoned all of the clients that he dealt with to check out their stories and their dealings with my friend and prospective partner and then heard all of what had really happened. Several clients told me that my friend had told them that I was opening a branch office and that he was going to run it for me, also requesting that they dealt with the new branch. Obviously a lie and I found out that he was meanwhile he was planning to go into partnership with another accountant friend of his and set up a new practice taking my clients.

I was both absolutely furious with him and totally amazed that someone could be as devious as that… Hey, but that how one learns. *"Experience is gained from things that go wrong… Not from things that go right!"* I decided that this had to end now and that I was going to sack him regardless of any consequences on the grounds of 'Serious Misconduct' and this I did with immediate effect. I asked for his company car back and sent him a formal letter of dismissal and hoped that it would be the end of a bad experience for all

My friend and possible partner had terminated all possibilities of a future hardly before it took root because of lies and deception; this was not however going to be the end of the matter. A few weeks later I received a communication from the Industrial Tribunals citing constructive dismissal and unfair dismissal by me.

I needed to take some decisive urgent action in the interests of the firm and after some thought, decided to write to every client simply saying that my friend had left the practice and that I had assumed responsibility for all clients personally once again; this action paid off because I only lost one single client who decided to go with him, under another name of course, some told me that they had been put under pressure to leave and join his other friend's practice, thankfully they remained loyal to me; it was damage limitation at its best.

In due course the notification of the Industrial Tribunal hearing came through and I had to prepare my case with all necessary documents and witnesses for my side of the case. I even prepared a letter of offer to him working out the profit of the business while he was there and offered him 50%

of the profit less his drawings to date, as we had initially agreed. I passed this offer to the conciliation service as well before the date of the hearing, to my surprise he rejected my offer and wanted to go on with the hearing. I had no idea what he was going to be claiming.

The first day of the hearing produced more surprises than I could have imagined, even though I had legal representation. The summary of it was that he said he had not signed any partnership agreement and was merely an employee and that I had paid him a salary as a manager and that my offer of a profit share was purely discretionary. I was totally surprised as to why he would want to reject my offer of almost twenty thousand pounds.

As the first days hearing went on it became clear that he wanted me to pay his Tax and National Insurance as an employee instead of paying his own tax as a self-employed partner on his share of the profit, which is the normal procedure in a partnership. When asked by the tribunal panel why he thought I was offering a 50% share of the profit he said that that was a discretionary bonus I wanted to pay him

He also made up a very elaborate story that I used to shout at him at our meetings and he was intimidated by me and was claiming that my suspending him was constructive dismal. I was appalled that someone who knew me for so long and had worked with me for fourteen months daily could stand a few yards away from me and make all this up, nevertheless this was what I had to face up to and defend my position. The hearing for the day had ended without either of us having to finish giving our evidence or examining each other's witnesses, therefore it was carried forward to another day about two weeks away.

I could also see that my lawyers and witnesses were no match for the street fight that he was waging and that their professionalism would lose me the case. I realised that I had to come up with something smarter to defeat the untruths he was saying. I went back to the office somewhat disappointed and decided that I needed to think laterally if I was to outsmart this guy.

The next day I thought about what he had said; and what I had offered him I decided to telephone the Inland Revenue to check what their position would be in both scenarios; one if I won the case and secondly if I lost the case, their answer was quite simple. If he was adjudged to be an employee, I would have to pay his Tax and National insurance and if I lost the case, they could still come after the practice for tax on his share of the profit. I calculated that the Tax and National Insurance would amount to about eighteen thousand pounds almost the same as they share of profit I had offered him.

After much thought, it became clear to me that I had to play him at his own game and turn the tables on him. I decided that as I could end up having to pay his tax anyway I should agree with him and accept that he was an employee and pay the PAYE tax and as he had already told the tribunal that any money I have offered him was a discretionary bonus, I would use my discretion to withdraw my offer and pay him a bonus of absolutely zero. I felt this was the best solution for me and I needed to communicate this to the panel of the Industrial Tribunal.

Accordingly, I wrote to them simply saying that I accepted what the plaintiff was saying and that I did not wish to waste any more of their time and would like to have their findings and decision in writing. Having discharged my lawyer, I attended the resumed hearing on my own and confirmed my position to the Tribunal panel, who confirmed receipt of my letter and new position, which they accepted. I had lost the case but won the day as my ex-friend had to accept the new position which was what he had sought. In due course I had the written ruling of the tribunal and duly paid his PAYE tax. I did not pay his profit share that I had offered him and the case was closed.

I need to record that about six months later I had a letter from a firm of lawyers telling me that they acted for my ex-friend and had been instructed to demand a sum of ten thousand pounds for damages and compensation and unpaid bonuses due to my nameless friend for the time he was employed by me. I simply wrote back to the lawyers sending them a copy of the Tribunal's findings and pointing out that no payment was due for anything. I also threatened them with a unspecified claim for damages to the practice and the reputation of the firm which could have gone into thousands of pounds. I never had any response to my threat of proceedings or ever heard from the other party again. I think that the case was finally at an end and although it did not cost my firm any extra money the cost of time for lost hours and stress from the all-consuming dispute was considerable. The phrase "keep your friends close and enemies even closer" began to mean a new reality to me.

I cannot end this episode without telling my readers that well after the end of the case I telephoned my ex-friend's previous employer and spoke to their managing director and asked him for a reference on my ex-friend. What he had to tell me totally astounded me when he said, "Your friend almost ruined this company and we were very lucky to get rid of him when we did, it has taken years to rebuild the damage he caused here." The business lesson that had to be learned is that no matter whom you employ and however well you know them never neglect to take the normal sensible precautions you would take irrespective of the relationship or friendship and make sure that all agreements are in writing, however brief they maybe; business is business and I could have saved a lot of heartache and money had I been more diligent about this.

15.

My Son Joins the Practice

The foregoing episode had left me somewhat disappointed in human nature and trust in other business practices, which was not the way in which I was educated and the fellowship of St Thomas' college, where we were brought up to do things with honour and where our word was our bond. This was an new life experience and one which would change my outlook forever – in life we deal with people from all walks of life and different ethical codes therefore, it is necessary to adapt to the ways of the world and make sure that one is prepared for all eventualities and the best way to do that is make sure that all agreements are in writing and good business practice is observed. I was not the first person who was rolled by a friend on the make and I wish I could say that I never made a similar mistake.

As I had mentioned earlier during all the years of my professional life and being an accountant, my eldest son Mark had decided that he wished to follow in my footsteps and choose accountancy as his career path, therefore as soon as he got his degree he decided to join one of the firms that I worked for and received my senior training in which to serve his apprenticeship and qualify. It was more or less a foregone conclusion that as soon as Mark qualified and was able to join me he would, Blick Rothenberg was a fine professional firm and the training he had there would more that equip him to join the practice and become a very useful addition to the team, furthermore as a fully qualified accountant he would give strength to the upper end of the business where I needed the greatest input. It was almost too long to wait but after the last lesson of getting a partner, I decided to be a little patient and wait until Mark was ready to join me.

In the meantime I expanded the second layer of the staff and took on more staff to service the client needs, also helping to train all of them to be focussed on delivery and quality of service. As I had trained and worked in the larger firms myself I had always been used to sound structure and the ethos of producing a quality service. The culture of planning, doing and reviewing was also not new to me so I was able to conduct this on an ongoing basis constantly reviewing the service we gave and reviewing it with improvements.

Finally it seemed that Mark was ready to make the move to leave Blick Rothenberg and join me in the practice. It was obviously an exciting event in that he was enthusiastic and the existing clients took to the idea of my son working with me to be a bonus as regards the service we were giving them and they did not always have to wait to see me.

Initially, we visited all the clients together so that I could introduce Mark to them and some may have even felt that as he was younger than me he may have been easier to communicate with, especially among the younger clients. The feedback was extremely good and the formula seemed to work well because we were able to grow the practice faster and offer a more comprehensive service. One of the best benefits was that Mark was able to carry out work himself with the clients rather than have consultations or visits from me. This produced a more in-depth relationship and opened the way to us offering a greater degree of service and opening the way to more sophisticated relationships with clients.

The arrangement gave a better distribution of the high end attention, because clients felt that seeing Mark was as good as seeing me and then we could also see them as a team. The arrangement worked well certainly in the first few years, although there were some problems of personality developing between us. I felt that Mark was competing with me and possibly resented the fact that clients did see me as the senior partner. I for my part always thought that we had very different personalities and different strengths and weaknesses in that he was a better 'Accountant' while I was a better 'Businessman' and this always seemed to upset Mark.

I was always very proud of his speed of thought and retentive memory and quickness with figures, but he seemed to prefer to want to be the lateral thinker which I think I have always been, partly because I was far more of a dreamer. The simple fact of the matter is that one is born with a set of skills and how we use them is up to us.

Many years later, Mark admits that I was right at the time and that we could have worked better as a team. Whenever we discuss these situations Mark says that I should have been a CEO of a much larger organisation rather than running a niche accountancy practice. The truth is that one does not always have full control of how things turn out in real life. In my experience of life its changes and the direction in which it takes up have always happen, rather than being fully planned.

I always reflect seeing an interview with David Mellor when he said… "Life is what happens to you while you are making other plans." It may well have been someone else's saying, but it has always meant something profound to me.

After a few years Mark started to feel that growth of an accountancy practice was a very slow way of accumulating wealth and he was more tempted by the idea of moving into property as a business and even suggested to me that we should sell the accountancy practice and use the capital to move into the property sector.

I was not tempted by this idea at all for many reasons, firstly I had founded the company over fifteen years earlier and I was considered by bankers and other professionals to be ideally suited to have a property portfolio as a secondary business, particularly as the accountancy business provided the security for property loans and mortgages. More so, because the eighties and nineties saw two very large property recessions and many property speculators bit the dust.

Among other reasons was that to me the firm and its success was now my life, whereas to Mark it was a business that he came into because of his father and to which he wasn't sentimentally attached. I daresay that he must have found my obsession with the firm and the clients quite irritating. In fact it was on one such evening when I phoned Mark well after hours and he simply said to me "Dad I'm having dinner and a glass of wine and I don't want to talk to you about work." To which I replied "Well in that case perhaps we should think about parting company." This I think was the beginning of the end of our partnership in accountancy.

Things dragged on from there for about another two years and although we worked successfully together in growing the practice and providing the services well to the clients, I don't think that Mark's heart was fully in the accountancy practice. I felt that the full formality and the discipline and the nature of the business was something he didn't enjoy, in honesty he was more interested in pulling deals. I once told him that he was like a footballer who hung around the goal mouth waiting to score a goal, whereas I was more of a mid-fielder helping the team to get there. There was a difference in expectation and interest in our approach to business and while we shared some aspects of our training and skills, there was a divergence of thought on how to get there. It eventually led to us deciding to go our separate ways in business.

Mark felt that he had helped grow the business to a higher degree and thought that he should be paid a share of the growth from the time he joined until he left as a capital sum apart from the salary and profit share he had derived from the business for the years that he had worked with me. I agreed that this was reasonable basis of settlement and we worked out the figures, which were used to settle the finances.

We did have a mutual interest in property and had a joint portfolio for many years after making a serious success on that front, but it was always a second string to my bow, while it was a primary interest to him. Strangely enough he is now in business with a professional colleague running a firm of chartered accountants, but still not as his primary interest.

16.

Moving Premises

The practice had moved into the premises in Marylebone and had been there since 1985 and needless to say we had cultivated a certain reputation in the area with other professionals, such as lawyers and bankers and other local businessmen who were keen to share mutual introductions and this we did on a regular basis. Most of all our clients regarded our offices as being somewhat prestigious and well located; this always adds an extra dimension to any business. I always put a huge emphasis on my 'shop window' and ensured that although we were a small firm our client areas looked impressive. In fact it matters more if you are a small firm because people often associate small firms with lower standards and this never happened to us because I made sure it did not. I always stressed to my staff that we as a team must strive for excellence in all our standards; this philosophy has paid off throughout the years.

However, the reality was that we simply needed more staff and consequently more space for people and storage and therefore after almost two years the search for new premises began. In the meantime I looked to merge with other similar firms in the immediate area and found a few possibilities and had begun initial negotiations with anyone suitable. One such firm was three times the size of us in terms of gross fees, and negotiations had begun in earnest. They were located close by to us and would have had space to house the resulting merged firm, in addition they had one majority partner and one minority partner which was identical to our set-up, I think it was fair to say that all parties concerned were extremely interested and agreed to get down to the nitty gritty practical issues of systems and profit shares of the 'New Merged Practice'. Having considered the way forward the excitement and anticipation fell apart because although we were the smaller firm our systems were well ahead of theirs and the senior partner was unable to come to terms with giving up part of his equity to the junior partners to make the merger work. My analysis of the situation was that accountants may be good at numbers, but mostly lacked the vision of being in business; they were too focussed on the bottom line rather than the potential of the new deal.

Having reached the situation of two possible suitable mergers but no obvious way forward, we sought larger premises in earnest. It was not an easy task because of the lack of business premises for sale and I have never been a believer in renting, then we suddenly came across a premises in Euston not too far away from Marylebone, with huge potential which was for sale because the incumbent wanted to sell the property but retain his practice; it was perfect for us.

The premises was quite large, all on one level and was available for immediate vacant possession. We completed the deal and bought the Euston Street office, I anticipated that it would serve us well for many years to come. The premises were already occupied by two sole traders in accountancy, one of whom was selling the premises and the other was keen to merge with us and stay on in the building. It so came about that we agreed terms and merged the two practices and although we stayed together for around eight years, a proper merger never took place. Our merger partner never wanted to change his modus operandi and still wanted to stick to his own software etc. It was only a matter of time before I told him that in view of his reluctance to change it made sense for him to simply take his clients and leave, this he did, and we were back to our original firm.

17.

The Merger

The merger between Ian Anthonisz and Co. and David Neville & Co was almost a text book exercise we decided that the name of the merged practice would be Anthonisz Neville LLP which remains the name even today. I constructed the arrangements as to the shares of the partners in the practice, the capital and current accounts and the negotiations went extremely well – we signed the actual Partnership Agreement in a relatively short time and the merger seemed to be full of promise. Unfortunately our new partner had his own way of doing things and was unable to compromise or change his long established working methods. My business partner Dawn and I were willing to look at what was best for the combined firm but this did not work, for many years the firm ran two sets of bookkeeping software, two sets of accounts preparation software and even two sets of payroll software. It was obvious that growth was impeded and the real benefits of the merger would never be achieved. We did have some cost savings in the professional indemnity cover and the costs of running the staff and office overhead costs, but these were minimal in the context of the entire firm. We were never able to achieve savings in the same staff working on the same system and in fact when the de-merger took place we managed with 50% of the entire staff, this tells us part of the story.

The lessons that one can learn from this misadventure is that mergers can never be forced and that the general ethos of the merging parties need to be similar; this is of course necessary in smaller organisations rather than in very large mergers where systems are forced on the smaller merging party as in the case of banks and similar industrial organisations.

Our merger could have been a great step forward for both of our firms had both parties really wanted to benefit from the shared expertise and the division of responsibilities between all the partners, rather than having two senior partners, two tax departments and so on. We felt the benefit in some of the areas but were unable to streamline the entire operation such as making economies in stationery supplies and the cost of accounting software, because neither of the two merged firms was willing to try the others. In our case we were using what was the best software on the market and were reluctant to step back to the other firm's software which in my opinion would have been a step backwards. Likewise David was unwilling to try our software because of the learning curve and the fact that his staff were used to their software. Generally speaking apart from the staff cost the biggest expense in an accountancy firm is the software licences and the staff operating the accounts preparation work, we therefore had double the software and staff cost. On reflection this should have been sorted out before we merged and I think that a combination of things led to this position. On the one hand David wanted to remain in the premises rather than relocate and I was extremely keen to buy the property including the tenant, this made for strange and unhappy bedfellows.

The situation dragged on for approximately seven years without either party making a firm stand until I decided that as no benefits of the merger were realised we may as well split up and go our separate ways. This we did and Anthonisz Neville LLP was born a much stronger and viable firm properly run by myself and Dawn my business partner. David had taken his clients and joined a much larger firm where he felt he would have the benefits of security of that firm and was possibly not interested in being part of the decision-making process of that firm. Either way we never remained in contact and one can only assume that he was happy with his position thereafter.

I was happy that I was once again fully in charge of our destiny and growth and once we had rationalised the staff and systems of operating the firm we concentrated on this process.

18.

A Second Setback

During the years of the merged firm we decided that we needed to employ a senior manager to supervise the audit and accounting teams and we interviewed and employed a person called Begitt, who we thought was extremely smart and would be the right man for the job and that he might also have partnership prospects in the long run.

The first few months proved to be most fruitful in this direction and we all worked well with him, clients and staff liked him equally and he had an air of knowledge and confidence about him. I also had an excellent rapport with him and we worked well together, I have to say that I had great hopes of him for the future of the firm.

In view of all his strong points I told him that it would make sense for him to bring any possible clients to the firm and that we would recognise any new clients introduced to the firm by paying him a commission on any fees earned and that he could do their work during normal working hours rather than do such work 'on the side' which would have been counterproductive to both of us, I also told him that in the event he left before he became a partner, he could take his clients with him. He agreed that this was a good idea and we prepared a memorandum of understanding to this effect.

All went well with Begitt for a considerable time. He by nature was a very social animal and each evening after five he would come to everyone's door and ask if we were interested in going out or joining him for a drink. Although I was not a habitual after-work drinker I sometimes indulged more for the sake of moral and promoting harmony with the staff rather than the idea of having any alcohol.

By now he was in charge of all the large audits and jobs and on one such evening outing I joined him and some other members of staff for drinks; we had what was a very enjoyable evening and carried on for longer than usual. At approximately 9:30 that evening I said that I would be leaving and told him that he should not have a hang over the next morning because we both had a very important meeting the next meeting with a client, he assured me that he would not!

The next morning I arrived at the office already mentally prepared for our meeting and got some of the papers ready while waiting for Begitt to come in.

The time passed and there was no sign of him so I decided to call him and find out what he was up to. I was extremely surprised and angered to find out that he had a big hangover and told me that he was unable to get to the office. In view of this sudden problem I decided to open his computer and print out the clients documents that I needed for the meeting. What I discovered surprised even more, there was a folder which said 'clients' and I opened this to see if the papers I was looking were there, only to find an empty folder other than another folder which said 'clients'. When I opened this folder I found a similar 'clients' folder and so the process went on for seven such folders. The seventh folder yielded the most amazing discovery I would make, there were over thirty client folders all of which were not known to us and Begitt had worked on all of them during the normal working days.

I had stumbled across our manager running what amounted to his own accountancy practice right under our noses in our time. To say that I was furious is an understatement. We had treated this guy so well offered him partnership prospects and accommodated him to bring in clients with financial participation and here he was cheating us and betraying our trust and good faith in him. I needed to take immediate, thoughtful action to get all the evidence I needed and to secure the information so that I could confront the situation correctly and protect the firm as well.

All this happened on a Friday morning and I had all weekend to research the depth of the betrayal an plan on a course of action to sort it out. I immediately called in our IT providers and asked them to download a security copy of the information I had discovered and lock his computer, in addition I got a print-out of all the information from his hidden folders. I also discovered that he was applying for other jobs using my CV made out to be his own. At this stage I decided not to tell Begitt about my discovery and armed with all this information that I had printed out I decided on a plan to confront him without warning.

Both my business partners, David and Dawn, were abroad on holiday at the time and I needed to deal with the situation on my own and without prior consultation with both of them. The plan I worked out was to have him go directly into the boardroom as he walked into the office on the Monday morning and I instructed my PA Abbey on what to do when he walked in. Abbey stood no more than five foot and built very small too and it was wonderful to watch this tiny woman confidently instruct Begitt to do just that. She said to him "Begitt, Ian wants to see you in the board room," and as he tried to brush past her into the general office she stretched both hands and blocked his way saying again "Into the boardroom please, Begitt." She was like a little Gurkha soldier, absolutely fearless. I was very impressed at the way she carried out her instructions, saw him into the boardroom and shut the door.

I kept him guessing as to the reason for our meeting for a few minutes and then slowly walked in armed with all my print outs.

I began by telling him that I had something extremely serious to talk to him about and that I wanted him to explain his behaviour as regards his terms of employment and his conduct to which he replied, "What is this all about?" I slowly and deliberately explained what I had discovered and how shocked I was about the discovery and wanted him to explain his behaviour.

He began by trying to say that it was all a misunderstanding and that he was going to introduce the clients to the firm and was desperately trying to cover his tracks. I then asked him about the CV he had prepared in his name using all my qualifications and experience and he simply denied it all. I thought that it was time to put all the printed out proof of what I had found in front of him and let him comment on it. When he saw what I put on the boardroom table he was dumbfounded and looked quite sheepish about everything. I think he realised that the game was up. I told him that I was going to suspend him with immediate effect with a view to dismissing him on the grounds of 'Serious Misconduct'.

I told him that he had to leave the premises without access to his computer and that I would get in touch with him in the next few days as I had to inform David and Dawn about the situation and the action I had taken. He then pleaded with me to have access to his emails only, I agreed but only under my supervision, which was a serious mistake on my part because Begitt was very IT savvy and as soon as he switched the computer on he tried to delete the firm's main server drive, as soon as I noticed what he was trying to do I leapt across the desk and switched the power off and told him that he had to leave without accessing his emails and that he had breached the goodwill I had offered him. His response was that I was breaching his human rights. I told him to go and see his lawyer and write to me about it, I escorted him to the door and ordered him out.

Whatever he did to the server it resulted in a partial failure of the main server and I had to call our IT providers to rectify the resulting problem at a cost to the firm of around £4,000 because the drive had been corrupted and each folder had to be retrieved individually from the backup drive. The lesson to be learned was that once an employee was suspended or dismissed they should never be allowed access to the IT systems and they could inflict unbelievable damage to the company's IT and backup files.

I contacted my partners Dawn and David in due course and updated them as to what had happened and how I had dealt with the matter and that I intended dismissing him for Gross Misconduct immediately, particularly after the computer incident, needless to say they were both in agreement with my actions.

As regards Begitt and his threatened actions, we never heard from him again, which indicates to me that he was guilty on all counts and had compounded the matter by his unsuccessful attempt to delete the main drive of the firm's file server. I have always maintained that in situations such as this there can be no alternatives other than to take the strongest possible action whatever the consequences, otherwise weak leadership arises, which in itself leads ultimately to a fall in standards and the quality of the management of the firm. I have always been a great believer in this and never subscribed to weak options. I don't believe that in the forty years that I have run the firm I have ever been guilty of it.

19.

The Birth of our Charity

I had not returned to Ceylon, now called Sri Lanka, for over twenty-four years after I first left the country; since then of course many of my cousins and other relations had themselves moved to Australia, Canada and the United States of America for very similar reasons that had led my family to emigrate that many years earlier. After this first visit in 1983, I returned again after a further nine years in 1992 and then about every five or six years because by now the so called thirty year war conducted by the, Liberation Tigers of *Tamil Eelam* (LTTE) a Tamil militant organization, the Tamil Tigers was seriously in progress and there were many incidents of suicide bombers and other shootings throughout the island, which made it a somewhat unsafe tourist destination.

During Christmas 2004, where I was completing a business visit to Sri Lanka, we were overtaken by one of the biggest national disasters ever to happen to the island of Sri Lanka. The Indian Ocean tsunami of 26th December 2004 was caused by an earthquake that was thought to have had the energy of 23,000 Hiroshima-type atomic bombs took place under the sea, near the west coast of Sumatra, the epicentre had a magnitude of 9.0.

The violent movement of the Earth's tectonic plates displaced an enormous amount of water, sending powerful shockwaves in every direction. The tectonic plates in this area had been pushing against each other and building pressure for what is thought to be for thousands of years.

According to the National Geographic Society, "It is thought that the rupture was over more than 600 miles long and displacing the seafloor by around thirty feet horizontally and several feet vertically, which as a result, moved trillions of tons of rock, causing the largest magnitude earthquake in around forty years."

Within hours of this earthquake, huge killer waves radiated from the epicentre and slammed into the coastlines of around eleven countries destroying many of them from Thailand to as far as East Africa. Sri Lanka was one such country to suffer horrendous damage and killing more than 30,000 people.

The tsunami hit Sri Lanka because it was on the main propagation axis, and then diffracted around the southern coast of the island, so that the southwestern coast was as greatly damaged as the eastern coast.

A tsunami can be made up of a series of waves and the first wave may not be the most dangerous because the tsunami 'wave train' can come in surges of five minutes to an hour apart and the cycle is marked by the repeated retreat and advance of the ocean. I had friends who went onto the seabed to check the struggling fish after the first wave never realising that a second wave would follow.

Despite the lag of time between the earthquake and the impact of the tsunami, nearly all of the victims were taken completely by surprise because there were no tsunami warning systems in place.

The Indian Ocean tsunami travelled as far as 3,000 miles to Africa and still arrived with sufficient force to kill people and destroy property. Many people in Sri Lanka reported that they saw animals fleeing for high ground minutes before the tsunami arrived and strangely enough very few animal bodies were found afterward.

Unaware of what was taking place and with all this as a background, we were having lunch with a dear friend from way back in my school days and with all his family on the 26th December, which was a brilliantly sunny day in Colombo, when we became aware of what was happening to the island and how it would change things for us. Strangely enough one of the topics of our lunchtime conversation was that there was a little amount of water creating a minor flood in the outskirts of Colombo.

Having finished lunch I suddenly saw that I had about six or seven missed calls from the UK on my mobile phone, which of course did not have the high tech advances of today. I was a little concerned that I had not heard them or answered my phone when I finally got through to my business partner I discovered that several of my friends and family in the UK had heard all about the tsunami in the east and heard of the huge devastation and loss of life in Sri Lanka and in view of my silence had presumed that we were among those who had perished in the tsunami and here we were in Colombo unaware of the developing tragedy to the nation.

Having come to terms with the immediate realisation of the situation, we proceeded to contact all our friends and family in the UK to tell them that we were alive and safe in Colombo.

It was not that good for many on the southwestern coast of the island because the sunny bright day had been interrupted with this huge wave which destroyed everything in its path, and worst of all was the second wave that killed many who were taking shelter from the flood of the first one, simply because they did not know that it was coming.

Our immediate attention was then turned to the survivors and the walking wounded from other areas of the island and sure enough there were many from all the coastal resorts on the southeast, not to mention the ones who had lost their lives and others who had just escaped. Our hotel in Colombo had opened its doors, corridors and spare rooms and even the gardens to the holidaymakers who had lost all their possessions and just escaped with their lives.

The aftermath of the wave was filled with stories of tragedies to individuals and families alike and of course stories of narrow escapes and almost fatal injuries, but the immediate problem was getting food, water and shelter to the survivors and as we were present decided to see what immediate help we could offer. This came in the form of food packs, water and of course money to assist whatever was being done on the ground. To say that the whole place was in turmoil was not an exaggeration; early reports spoke of the numbers of dead and injured without really knowing the full extent of it and we discovered that help was pouring in from all over the world. In all such situations there were all the 'Fake' appeals to watch out for. I believe that many fake websites and charities were established and people were donating at stations, supermarkets and streets in many Western countries too.

It was in this turmoil that I decided that Janice and I would take a tour of the south of the island to find out for ourselves what had really happened. The results were absolutely horrifying. Cars and trains twisted and off the road and train tracks, houses and hotels washed away to the foundations and fishing boats up on trees and roofs of stronger buildings, almost impossible to imagine.

The first of the gigantic waves caused by the earthquake to hit this part of the island near Telwatta hit a crowded train which came to a halt as water surged around it. Hundreds of locals, believing the train to be secure on the rails, climbed onto the top of the cars to avoid being swept away. Others stood behind the train, hoping it would shield them from the force of the water. The first wave flooded the carriages and caused panic amongst the passengers. Ten minutes later a huge second wave picked the train up and smashed it against the trees and houses which lined the track, crushing those seeking shelter behind it. The eight carriages were so packed with people that the doors could not be opened while they filled with water, drowning almost everyone inside as the water washed over the wreckage several more times. The passengers on top of the train were thrown clear of the uprooted carriages and most drowned or were crushed by debris.

The locomotive was carried about 100 metres, coming to rest in a swamp. Both the engineer and his assistant died at their posts. Estimates based on the state of the shoreline and a high-water mark on a nearby building place the tsunami twenty-four to twenty-nine feet above sea level, and six to nine feet higher than the top of the train.

Having witnessed all these scenes of devastation and especially when looking out at the totally calm sea in the radiant sunshine, it is impossible to relate what had happened when looking out at the sea from the coastline. I will always remember it was almost too much to take in the eerie silence and the calmness of the sea and the helpless feeling that out of the silence and depth could come another wave of destruction. I also wondered if I would ever feel comfortable sleeping in a hotel or house near the sea again or if I could one ever trust the power and might of the silent sea and waves.

I have always been criticised by my and friends and family of making decisions too quickly and impulsively and it was in one such moment that I decided that I needed to do something about people who had been affected by this tragedy and had lost everything. Thus the idea of my starting a charity was born.

Immediately on our return to London we met with our long time close friends Colin and Rosemarie Colin for coffee and related to them our experiences. It was an emotional story and after filling them in with the smallest details of the tsunami and our experiences there, I told them what I was planning to do. Almost without hesitation Colin said, "Ian I have always wanted to do something for mankind myself but never had the opportunity to start this, therefore, I would like to join you in the project."

Without saying much more about it the Once in a Lifetime Charity (OIAL) was born, with myself, Janice, Colin and Rosemarie being the trustees of a charity that pledged 100% of any donations we received would go to our causes. For my part I had an idea of how to raise the initial funds which was to write to all my clients and friends in my address book and tell them that I was starting a charity with an initial donation of £1,000, and invited everyone I knew and wrote to join me in matching the donation or whatever they felt they could give, the result was extraordinary, we collected near on £60,000, an unimaginable and humbling experience.

All four of us returned to Sri Lanka to survey how we could practically use the funds to rebuild the lives of some of the people affected by the wave. It is worthwhile to mention that neither Colin nor Rosemarie had ever been to Sri Lanka and to their credit they got stuck in from the very moment we got there.

We helped several of the families that had been directly affected by the tsunami these ranged from helping a young boy – who had lost his entire family while he was selling produce at a fair when the wave struck and his entire family, save a younger sister, were completely washed away without any trace – by giving him a tractor to take his produce to the market; to building a house for a fisherman and his family, who had lost their house and his fishing boat. Most of all we used the motto of "Teach a man to fish and you will feed him for the rest of his life" rather than give any handouts.

OIAL is a small charity and unlike the big charities and others we all agreed that none of us would use any of the funds to pay for any travel or other expenses on ourselves, allowing us therefore to use all the donations on our causes, a value we still hold today and has proved to be extremely popular among our donors, especially now after some of the scandals that have been exposed in the large charities.

I need to say that after a few years we saw that some of the tsunami victims had now become the 'tsunami rich' in

Sri Lanka, which in our opinion is because so many in the entire Western world poured in so much help and financial support without making any proper checks, and encouraged the greedy local population to make many fictitious and exaggerated claims of losses, that they now had more than they ever had before the wave struck, such is human greed.

We then decided to change our causes to poor and impoverished people who had very little or nothing to speak of and I am pleased to say that our project has been running very successfully for over twelve years since early 2005 and I cannot fully describe how humbling and emotional the journey has been so far.

Among our achievements, we have built six nursery schools and helped over 1,200 families to improve their living conditions by having really simple improvements to their homes such as giving them a watertight roof, a kitchen or a toilet – something that we in the west absolutely take for granted.

We have built over six deep water wells in areas of drought for the use of all the villagers in the areas and have provided water tanks for the use of the community. I have always felt that water is something required for basic living and it is every person's right to be able to have access to it. Poorer countries always suffer from a lack of clean usable water. Personally, I never use bottled water if I can possibly avoid it.

Among our causes we help disabled people who have lost a limb or limbs due to snake bites, diabetes and in some cases having fallen from trees or suffered an accident; we work in conjunction with the Colombo Friend in Need Society, who provide artificial limbs, and we sponsor people who need arms or legs to get help from them.

We also sponsor individuals or families who through illness or accident are living in dire circumstances to bring about some kind of improvement to their lives. An illustration of two of these are Mallika who has twins aged around three and lost her husband in an accident, with no means of a livelihood, we have sponsored the two girls with a monthly allowance which gives them a better quality of life.

Another such case is the case of Sirimi who lost both legs due to diabetes and had enormous difficulty with her toilet and bathroom facilities, we had a disabled bathroom built in her home with hand rails in the toilet and shower to help her with an easier life, simple and effective.

Nothing of this would have been possible without the amazing generosity of our donors I therefore need to say thank you with all sincerity and humility and acknowledge

I would like to invite all my readers in all humility to visit the charity website to truly get a feel of our achievements to date, rather than try to list them (www.oialcharity.org).

I would also like to use this opportunity to dedicate this chapter of the book to the extreme generosity of all the donors to the Once in a Lifetime charity project and to mention that "Your generosity and support has been simply overwhelming and the most humbling experience of our lives." In recognition of this I plan to donate 10% of the sales receipts of this book to the Once in a lifetime charity

20.

The Sell by Date...

I have always believed that any and every business has a value and as long as it has been groomed for that it will always have a sales price. The value would range depending on its earning potential but anything from a small shop to and accountancy practice has profitability, and this is therefore the primary factor in determining its worth. I have always been aware of this and had noticed that people, especially professionals, have always thought that their business was only worth anything to themselves and not worth anything to sell outside. The result was that they ran the business until they wanted to retire or stop at which time it simply ceased trading, alternatively as they got older someone took over and paid them a small amount for goodwill.

In all the years I have been in business I have arranged many sales of my clients businesses to outsiders or even other clients, most of them convinced that they had nothing to sell. It does however take lots of preparation and planning in order to achieve the maximum price. It is also my view that like anything there is an optimum date at which to achieve this, otherwise the date passes and the bargaining position fails, as it does on a property transaction where a buyer or a seller gets too greedy or is not prepared to be flexible enough to achieve a deal.

With these thoughts in mind I had always thought that unless there was a scenario of natural succession, such as one of both of my sons taking over the practice, I would prepare to sell the practice when I was ready to give up playing the lead role, but most certainly when I was still being perceived as the top man in the business rather than being perceived as getting past it. In mind there were several reasons for this. I would have hated clients or other business associates turning to someone else instead of me for opinions or advice or my fellow professionals thinking that I was getting past my best.

Both my sons, who themselves were qualified chartered accountants, had expressed the view that they did not want to be in practice with me or that there were interested in being in public practice at all, this left me with some very clear alternatives both to securing my financial future and also dictated the path which I should take to ensure this happens.

There are of course several ways of structuring a partner's exit from a firm; one of the ways to leave a practice beneficially is to merge with another firm which is capable of buying out a retiring partner at a fixed future date, normally this gives the junior partners a greater share of the equity, or one or more of the existing partners buys the retiring partner out.

I had explored the merger possibility on several occasions and found it to be one of the most difficult things to achieve, especially with smaller firms for several reasons.

In my experience I found with the smaller firms generally they were travelling forward at different speeds because the senior partners had different approaches to growth, technology, equity shares and what they were willing to part with in the general good. On two occasions I found that although we were the smaller firm we were well ahead on all fronts compared with the larger potential merger partner. In one case our systems, software and computer technology were so far ahead that the larger firm would have needed to have about six months to catch up with us, this is not a great start and undermines the negotiations at most stages.

In my negotiations with the much larger firms, where it was more of a takeover rather than a merger, I always found that they always wanted to dictate terms rather than negotiate and this generally led to a breakdown, unless you were willing to simply give up your brand and individuality in favour of the larger partner. In my case this was not something I was willing to do simply because I had invested almost forty years in a brand and a philosophy of service to our clients. Our original brochure boasted the motto

> **"Developing the Ultimate Business Partnership with our Clients."**

And also claimed that our services were

> **"Aimed at the discerning client who prefers individual attention."**

It was something that I as the founder treasured and instilled in all our staff and tried to fulfil from the very early days until now. Naturally, I was unwilling to simply discard this approach to business to maximise fees at the cost of decreased service to our clients.

After about ten years of running the practice I had structured the office in such a way that it could run effectively without my daily input, although I was very hands-on as regards the quality of the staff and the work we produced, and took the leadership of running the practice together with client liaison as my main task. Looking back it was obviously a strategy that was correct and it paid off.

Having considered the available alternatives I decided that the best path for me to follow was to offer my partner to buy my share of the equity out, her immediate response was that she could not afford it, this was not surprising to me at all because I have always found that unless you are a risk taker, which all entrepreneurs need to be, the idea of buying something without the ready funds is quite a scary exercise. The difference is that an entrepreneur looks at the deal and if they think it is a viable proposition they will set about the options of raising the funds to complete the deal. I knew that the business was extremely sound it had been going for almost forty years and it gave several people a good living, apart from which it would always have a fall back capital value. Knowing this, I set about trying to convince my partner of these facts, not simply because they were true but I felt that someone who had worked for so many years, knew the business, knew the clients, the systems and everything about it was in a better position to take it over and grow it to their benefit, apart from which I would be available in almost any role to support and assist the new ownership as required.

With this end in sight I set about working out the figures that would convince my partner that it would be an amazing opportunity for her to capitalise on the work she had put in over the years, rather than have me sell to an outside buyer who may have bypassed or side-lined her in their own growth plans after my departure. Having worked out the value of the business and the method in which she could buy my equity it remained my task to convince her that it was correct and that it was a very real opportunity for her and although it took me several months to convince her, she eventually realised that I was correct in my analysis and that it was a totally feasible proposition both as a business and as to its affordability, we then set about making the necessary arrangements to complete the deal.

In the meantime I had investigated the possibility of selling to an outside buyer but declined all the offers I had because they all wanted to buy me out but pay later – most unrealistic simply because they could ruin one's business in two years or the payment method in my opinion were flawed. The reason for this I discovered is that by and large accountants are really not businessmen and when they approach a business deal they think like accountants and not as businessmen. This is not to say that all accountants are the same, there are many who can wear the different hats that of a businessman and that of a technical figure guy and in my view these are the guys who are really successful and generally go on to build business empires.

The negotiations continued with my business partner until it was concluded to the satisfaction of both of us. The ambition I had set myself had been achieved.

21.

Other Interests...

I think that it is fair to say that throughout my life I was always interested in business ventures; it is almost like I was born with this trait and as a very young boy whenever I mentioned these thoughts in the company of adults they always thought that I was a crazy child who was a total dreamer. I am convinced however that it is that interest that helped me to get where I wanted to be. As a young boy I was always buying and selling, even my toys and play items, to family and friends alike, this began to get more serious when I got to the age of owning a bicycle. I repeated the process by buying a cheap one cleaning it, painting it and selling it for a profit until eventually I was able to buy the one I wanted.

When I think back I did this as young adult selling radios, model cars and aeroplanes to my brother and cousins or close friends. I always admired the risk takers in business and was interested in the way they operated; the big entre- preneurs of the day for me were people like Charles Forte, Charlie Clore, and later on Freddie Laker and Richard Branson. I idolised their flair and commercial enterprise and in my own way saw myself being one of them, although this never materialised, in the same sense.

I once said to my bank manager that when I compared myself to these people I felt really past it and I remember him saying: Ian why do you compare yourself to the Richard Branson's of this world compare yourself to your own contemporaries and you will see that you have not done too badly... words of good sense.

I used the accident compensation I received for the car crash to buy my first property and of course this put me ahead of the game with all my fellow trainees and articled clerks, which meant that I owned my first property at around twenty-three years old. In the years that followed I always used any spare funds I had investing in 'Penny Shares' probably something quite odd for a twenty-three-year-old young man, but that was me always looking for a deal with an eye to making a profit.

Once I had started business on my own and had established good banking connections I was able to expand my interest of a side-line of investment in the property market. My strategy was relatively simple in that I borrowed funds on an interest only repayment which meant that I repaid the capital borrowing only on the sale of the property. This gave me a huge cashflow advantage as there was no capital repayment and the repayments were quite reasonable when compared to the potential income. During the last twenty years the property market has kept on growing, despite the odd drop in the market, therefore it was difficult to lose money.

In addition, I preferred to buy my office premises rather than rent because I felt that rental was wasted money and preferred to buy and pay a loan or mortgage because in cashflow terms there was hardly any difference but the capital growth was likely to be higher, I am aware that many people disagree with my strategy however during my business life it appears to have served me extremely well and I made some useful profits on every move of offices.

Furthermore, I always thought that if I owned the office the rental income would serve me as a good source of income after I retired or sold the business. This may not be everyone's reasoned strategy but it was certainly mine.

After my son Mark joined the business he shared my view and we went on to expand a joint property folio which we ran very successfully for many years. The general strategy was to purchase more properties during any downturns in the market and gradually sell as and when the market recovered, a strategy that seems to have paid off for us anyway, even after all the tax payments.

Towards the approach of the year 2000 I felt that it was an opportune time to invest in a software project as there was a massive growth and buzz about the millennium, and it was certainly the time of the dotcom boom. I was not an IT person nor was I an expert in IT programs. However I had an adequate knowledge of accounting and was sufficiently computer-literate to design some accounting software with the end user in mind.

To my mind most IT programs that were around were somewhat complicated and catered to the trained accountants, whereas I thought that a simple easy to use piece of software would be most useful, especially as I had observer that most small businesses and sole traders had their books written up by their mothers, girlfriends or a friend of the family rather than any qualified or experienced bookkeeper.

With this thought in mind, I decided to have a program that was easy to understand, simple to use and would be extremely affordable. My target market was to be the average small business or sole trader rather than a trained bookkeeper. In the UK alone there was a potential market of around one million and my reasoning was that I only wanted a very small percentage of that market to be users of my simple accounting software package.

Having met with a software developer I explained my project and the overall requirement, which was to be simple with easy to understand language and graphics which would make the program very easy to use. The meetings went well and the amount of capital at risk, although considerable was manageable and worth the commercial risk in my view.

Having decided to go for the package, 'Easy Money Manager' was to be the name and I worked together with the developers to make it a reality. The project took a few years to complete and it seemed that it would be a bestseller because everyone I showed it to was very impressed and thought that it was extremely good value.

I had also offered my business partners in the accountancy practice a share of the ownership but they both turned me down because they did not wish to take a financial risk, therefore it became my accounting programme and my sole risk.

Once the program was completed I got fully into the package should look like and how it was to be sold, all of this was a totally new concept to me and I was determined to compete with all the other packages on the market.

I feel that I should show what the package and the concept of the finished program looked like therefore I have set out two pictures of the simple marketing leaflet looked like with the following illustrations:

Easy Money Manager

www.easymoneymanager.org

Support:

There is free telephone support for the first 30 days, after purchase.

After this period there are 3 different types of support for you to choose from:
1. **Telephone support** (@ £50 p.a. OR by Premium rate calls: 0905 757 0192 @ 0.95p per minute).
2. **On-line support** (available via e-mail @ £36 per annum).
3. **Tutorial support** (one to one attention, sessions are one hour long, cost £35.25 per hour).

Contact information:

1 Wesley Street
Marylebone
London
W1G 8LT

Phone: 44 (0) 207 388 6462
Fax: 44 (0) 207 935 8539
E-mail: info@easymoneymanager.org

Website: www.easymoneymanager.org

Take control of your money Now!

The Money Management System

Simple record keeping for Personal or Business Use.

Very easy to use
Simple reports
Fully supported
Unbeatable value for money

Easy Money Manager© - (EMM)

EMM is a simple money management system, designed for use by individuals and businesses.

It is not just another "accounting nightmare", because it is so simple to use.

✓ Created for those with little or no accounting or office experience
✓ The screens and wording are simple
✓ You will be able to follow the program in a matter of minutes
✓ Reports are easy to read and functional

Save on Accountancy Fees and Bank Charges!

All you have to do is:
• Set-up your user details and your bank account,
• Enter transactions (payments & receipts),
• You can reconcile your bank + check charges,
• View reports to find out the state of your finances.

The screens are simple and clear

Personal Version- Easy Money Manager - (EMM)

The product is based on Receipts (Income) and Payments (Expenses), Names, Dates and Amounts. Easy Money Manager has 14 separate record books, which can be used for bank accounts, cash accounts, mortgage accounts or even credit card accounts. Once the data has been entered the program summarises the transactions. You are then able produce reports based on the information you have entered. The reports show all the receipts or payments of individual categories or a summaries of multiple categories for any range of dates. It gives you all the information you need in a simple and clear format. It could not be easier!

Professional Version- Easy Accounts

This version of Easy Money Manager also incorporates a VAT facility, therefore it is more useful for businesses. The program provides concise information for accountants and can achieve a huge saving of fees on routine work.

Costs:
➢ Personal Version (Single User)- cost £49.50 - (P&P)*
➢ Professional Version (Includes 2 User Licences)- cost £79.50 - (P&P)
➢ Additional User- Licence Upgrade- cost £39.50

Compares unbelievably with other products, which range from £40 - £500, and are far too complicated to use!!!

SPECIAL OFFER!!!!
Buy now for only £39 per user on any version

Having completed the program, I held seminars and invited all the bank managers I knew individually in the hope that one of the banks would be interested in giving a copy of the software to their customers as a freebee to help them keep their records. I was surprised to find out that although there was a basic interest many banks had already tied up with other software producers.

One bank did show interest and wanted to have 10,000 copies at £9.95 a copy for distribution to their clients and although negotiations went a long way we never closed a deal, which could have recovered all my costs and made a good profit. I went on to sell several hundred copies of the program and although it was not a financial disaster, I never recovered my original outlay.

Nevertheless, I have valued the experience of taking a package from a concept to completion right through until it was a full on the shelf product... *"An Invaluable Experience."*

Software had moved on so much that although I had designed an online version to be brought out last year, I'm not sure that it will be successful at the moment. I have therefore decided to hold my horses for the time being because any program I bring out will have to be simple to operate and fulfil the competitive pricing required to compete with the big boys in the field.

Having said that I feel that there is a great future in IT and software because this is where technology is headed. I am extremely interested in being inventive and have designed a search platform which is almost complete, hopefully this will be unveiled in the next few months and hopefully will be a commercial success, which is never guaranteed but one will never know unless it is tried, so watch this space...

22.

Thoughts and Reflections

It is over forty years since I founded the accountancy practice of Anthonisz Neville LLP and I am pleased to say that it is going well and although a smaller niche firm, it has a very respected and recognised reputation and having being in business as long we have find that recommendatiòns is our largest source of new clients.

In recent years I have concentrated my work effort on clients who need or would like to have a business mentor or need coaching and would find my years of experience in business and the profession useful in building their own businesses, and it is something that I enjoy doing. I have reached a very comfortable work and life balance, particularly as it leaves me enough time to devote to our charity, "Once in a Lifetime". Apart from which the practice is run extremely efficiently by my business partners, Dawn and Chris.

Looking back over the time I have been in business and my professional life there are many things that I would like to reflect on; I have to say that in all the years I have never lost my passion for what I wanted to do which was to provide the best quality attention for the discerning client at the most realistic cost, certainly not the cheapest but I would like to think it was the best value for money.

I have always thought that nobody could run an organisation of any type or size without the passion they needed to do this well, as for myself I think this is an absolute necessity. In all the years that I worked based in the office, I was always the first person in and the last person out, such was my passion for the company.

I still believe in having a dream and a vision for anything that one wants to achieve without a dream or a vision how would one want to know where to get to, furthermore Walt Disney's saying of **"If you can dream it you can do it"** still holds true for me, as one's imagination is only limited by their own mind. It was a lesson I was made aware of when I first visited Disneyland in 1981 and during a recent visit to Disneyworld I discovered that the success of that organisation has been their inventiveness and their ability to reinvent themselves to stay ahead of the game.

Out of the values that we acquired during our education at St Thomas' College, something I valued throughout my life was integrity. I need to mention that on many occasions I have been completely humbled by the behaviour of people I met and knew and some who were clients of the firm, and although it would not be appropriate to mention any of the client stories, I cannot let the opportunity pass to mention two stories of friends of the family to illustrate the point.

Isabell was a friend of my mother's from her school days and I had seen her a few times at church chatting to my mother, but otherwise had no previous contact with her. One day my mother called me and told me that Isabell wanted to see me privately at her house; I arranged to go there subsequently and was more than somewhat taken aback when she presented me with a paper bag full of cash, which represented her life savings, many thousands of pounds. She gave me the bag and told me she wanted me to take care of it for her and that she would tell me what she wanted me to do with it at some future time. As I was totally unprepared for this scenario I took out my notebook to give her a temporary handwritten receipt until I was able to give her something more official, either way she would not hear of any such thing, she insisted that it was done on complete trust and I was charged with telling no one as she wanted it kept totally confidential, not even my mother her friend, she did not want it invested or any such thing just safeguarded until she wanted it and she would tell me when.

I was both amazed and totally humbled that someone trusted me with their lifesavings more than any member of their own family. Isabell assured me that she trusted me totally and I was not to worry at all. Since that day she would call me from time to time and ask me to pop in to see her and on each such occasion would give me more cash to be added to the original sum; I kept a meticulous note of everything with dates and amounts etc., she never wanted to know about my records and did not want a copy for herself.

Suddenly one day some years later I had a call from her asking me to come to a hospital to visit her as she was unwell. When I got there and asked her how she was, she asked me if I had my notebook to which I replied "Yes." She said Ian, I'm dying, and I want you to write down what I want you to do with the money I gave you to look after and she listed out the names of her daughter and grandson and their addresses and told me that when she died I was to contact them and give them the amounts as dictated by her. She finished the conversation by saying "You must be busy so go back to work and I trust you to carry out my wishes." Isabell passed away some time later and I contacted her family members as requested and did as I was instructed, surely one of the most humbling experiences of my life.

The other story that I still recall with amazement is when someone I will call 'Nonie' for the purpose of this story came to me to tell me that she had been diagnosed with breast cancer and was going to be admitted to a clinic the next day and wanted me to look after her life savings of more than £250,000, which at the time was a huge amount of money, again she would not take a receipt and simply said I trust you totally and I don't want any paperwork from you. Of course again I kept meticulous records of all monies in and out because she charged me with paying the hospital bills for her treatment and other medical needs. This arrangement carried on for several years, I insisted that she signed each withdrawal for the sake of my own records and comfort and to ensure there could never be any doubt as to the use of her money, she did so reluctantly because she thought it was unnecessary. Nonie recovered from her cancer after treatment and many years of checks and follow ups and I'm pleased to say is still around after more than twenty-five years. Once she had recovered from her illness I insisted that she should take the still large amount of her capital fund as it was an extremely onerous position to be in, she agreed reluctantly. Again I found it to be a very humbling experience that someone would trust me to this extent, but the truth is that it is quite an honour to be trusted to that degree.

I have been asked by some if I had any regrets or what mistakes I may have made in my business life. I have to say that there have been a few, the biggest one I think was that when I knew my eldest son was going to follow in my footsteps and make a career in accountancy, I allowed this to cloud my judgement and not take a qualified business partner to help grow the business in the early years when the growth potential was probably at its highest. I was reluctant to do this because I was waiting for my son Mark to qualify and join me in the practice; this was definitely a silly mistake on my part.

Firstly it set back the growth and as eventually proved he decided not to make it his chosen career. The lesson that I Learned was that one cannot decide what career path their children would follow nor can you decide your future based on that. I clearly should have done what I should have done for the needs of the firm at the time.

My message to any would be entrepreneurs is to always have a dream and vision of where you wish to get to rather than allow the possible profit you are going to make out of the venture to be your guide, if the venture is worth doing and you have the passion for it, success will follow and it's the success of the project which makes it financially viable. If you start with thinking how much you will sell you will be reluctant to start anything. The example I use frequently is that people should never start a coffee shop because there are so many already, but if you have noticed wherever there is a Starbucks there is also a Prets and a Costa and a Café Nero have you ever wondered why? It is simply because they all cater for different tastes and likes and they all seem to make a healthy profit. Somewhere there is a lesson – in business a better product and a better service will always attract new customers and take some of the others either on price or service.

Always try to think laterally, you may remember that earlier in this book I mentioned the notice behind Lord Victor Mishcon's chair which said **'It Can be Done'**. I always took this to heart and whenever faced with what I thought was an impossible situation I tried to think around it, most times the thinking would come up with a solution. I fondly remember when an American lawyer who was a great friend of mine told me that I was definitely not just an accountant but "a problem solver"; at first I wasn't sure what he meant but realised soon after that it was quite a compliment.

When I decided to write this book many people told me that I probably would not sell many copies, that may well be true but on that basis one would never do anything. I felt I needed to do it because I had a story to tell and there was a sense of achievement that I felt I needed to accomplish – as to whether it will be a commercial success, who knows? As far as I am concerned it is something I wanted to do for myself and can only hope for the rest and best!

Lightning Source UK Ltd.
Milton Keynes UK
UKHW020029200421
382255UK00007B/397